THIS IS YOUR **PASSBOOK®** FOR ...

SECRETARY I

NATIONAL LEARNING CORPORATION®
passbooks.com

COPYRIGHT NOTICE

This book is SOLELY intended for, is sold ONLY to, and its use is RESTRICTED to individual, bona fide applicants or candidates who qualify by virtue of having seriously filed applications for appropriate license, certificate, professional and/or promotional advancement, higher school matriculation, scholarship, or other legitimate requirements of educational and/or governmental authorities.

This book is NOT intended for use, class instruction, tutoring, training, duplication, copying, reprinting, excerption, or adaptation, etc., by:

1) Other publishers
2) Proprietors and/or Instructors of «Coaching» and/or Preparatory Courses
3) Personnel and/or Training Divisions of commercial, industrial, and governmental organizations
4) Schools, colleges, or universities and/or their departments and staffs, including teachers and other personnel
5) Testing Agencies or Bureaus
6) Study groups which seek by the purchase of a single volume to copy and/or duplicate and/or adapt this material for use by the group as a whole without having purchased individual volumes for each of the members of the group
7) Et al.

Such persons would be in violation of appropriate Federal and State statutes.

PROVISION OF LICENSING AGREEMENTS. — Recognized educational, commercial, industrial, and governmental institutions and organizations, and others legitimately engaged in educational pursuits, including training, testing, and measurement activities, may address request for a licensing agreement to the copyright owners, who will determine whether, and under what conditions, including fees and charges, the materials in this book may be used them. In other words, a licensing facility exists for the legitimate use of the material in this book on other than an individual basis. However, it is asseverated and affirmed here that the material in this book CANNOT be used without the receipt of the express permission of such a licensing agreement from the Publishers. Inquiries re licensing should be addressed to the company, attention rights and permissions department.

All rights reserved, including the right of reproduction in whole or in part, in any form or by any means, electronic or mechanical, including photocopying, recording, or by any information storage and retrieval system, without permission in writing from the Publisher.

Copyright © 2021 by

National Learning Corporation

212 Michael Drive, Syosset, NY 11791
(516) 921-8888 • www.passbooks.com
E-mail: info@passbooks.com

PUBLISHED IN THE UNITED STATES OF AMERICA

PASSBOOK® SERIES

THE *PASSBOOK® SERIES* has been created to prepare applicants and candidates for the ultimate academic battlefield – the examination room.

At some time in our lives, each and every one of us may be required to take an examination – for validation, matriculation, admission, qualification, registration, certification, or licensure.

Based on the assumption that every applicant or candidate has met the basic formal educational standards, has taken the required number of courses, and read the necessary texts, the *PASSBOOK® SERIES* furnishes the one special preparation which may assure passing with confidence, instead of failing with insecurity. Examination questions – together with answers – are furnished as the basic vehicle for study so that the mysteries of the examination and its compounding difficulties may be eliminated or diminished by a sure method.

This book is meant to help you pass your examination provided that you qualify and are serious in your objective.

The entire field is reviewed through the huge store of content information which is succinctly presented through a provocative and challenging approach – the question-and-answer method.

A climate of success is established by furnishing the correct answers at the end of each test.

You soon learn to recognize types of questions, forms of questions, and patterns of questioning. You may even begin to anticipate expected outcomes.

You perceive that many questions are repeated or adapted so that you can gain acute insights, which may enable you to score many sure points.

You learn how to confront new questions, or types of questions, and to attack them confidently and work out the correct answers.

You note objectives and emphases, and recognize pitfalls and dangers, so that you may make positive educational adjustments.

Moreover, you are kept fully informed in relation to new concepts, methods, practices, and directions in the field.

You discover that you arre actually taking the examination all the time: you are preparing for the examination by "taking" an examination, not by reading extraneous and/or supererogatory textbooks.

In short, this PASSBOOK®, used directedly, should be an important factor in helping you to pass your test.

SECRETARY I

DUTIES

Under general supervision, performs a variety of secretarial duties and administrative tasks for one or more professional or management positions, requiring some independence in interpreting departmental procedures and the point of view of the person served; performs related duties as required.

Performs tasks which fall into four broad categories: communication, coordination, organization and records maintenance. Within these categories, you would perform a variety of tasks which enable managers and program staff to accomplish the mission of the agency. You would review incoming correspondence and draft responses where appropriate; review outgoing correspondence; research background information; transmit instructions to staff and conduct follow-up. You would handle telephone calls and visitors and respond to questions; coordinate and arrange meetings; establish office procedures; design office filing systems; resolve day-to-day operational problems; coordinate information flow by acting as liaison among key executives, staff, other employees, and the public; and operate equipment which requires the manipulation of a standard alpha-numeric keyboard to produce correspondence, reports, and other agency documents.

EXAMPLES OF WORKS:
Duties may include, but are not limited to, the following:
- Composes brief, factual correspondence following general directions or notes.
- Type's letters, reports, numerical and technical material and minutes from draft, shorthand, or recorded dictation; takes dictation as required.
- Proofs and corrects material for grammar, punctuation, spelling, accuracy, format, and conformance to administration policy.
- Screens and directs mail arid calls; provides information requiring some interpretation of procedures and the supervisor's viewpoint.
- Keeps supervisor's calendar and makes appointments as directed; makes travel arrangements and prepares expense reports.
- Searches for specific material and compiles reports as instructed.
- Keeps and maintains files, logs and records, including budget, personnel and payroll records.
- Schedules meetings and conferences; prepares materials and agenda; may represent supervisor at meetings; takes, transcribes and distributes minutes.

- Relieves supervisor of administrative detail such as checking time and attendance reports and approving purchase requisitions
- Trains or orients new employees; may assign and review the work of others.
- Provides vacation and temporary relief as required.
- Opens, reviews, sorts and distributes mail in accordance with staff assignments;
- Reviews incoming correspondence and reports to determine their significance, makes recommendations to manager or refers to appropriate person for reply;
- Answers the telephone, responds to questions concerning program, policy or procedures and refers most complex technical questions to appropriate staff member;
- Schedules meeting and maintains calendar;
- May supervise clerical staff.

SCOPE OF THE WRITTEN TEST
The written test will be designed to test for knowledge, skills, and/or abilities in such areas as:
1. Understanding and interpreting written material;
2. Preparing written material;
3. Keyboarding practices;
4. Office practices;
5. Office record keeping; and
6. Grammar; usage; punctuation; spelling.

HOW TO TAKE A TEST

I. YOU MUST PASS AN EXAMINATION

A. WHAT EVERY CANDIDATE SHOULD KNOW

Examination applicants often ask us for help in preparing for the written test. What can I study in advance? What kinds of questions will be asked? How will the test be given? How will the papers be graded?

As an applicant for a civil service examination, you may be wondering about some of these things. Our purpose here is to suggest effective methods of advance study and to describe civil service examinations.

Your chances for success on this examination can be increased if you know how to prepare. Those "pre-examination jitters" can be reduced if you know what to expect. You can even experience an adventure in good citizenship if you know why civil service exams are given.

B. WHY ARE CIVIL SERVICE EXAMINATIONS GIVEN?

Civil service examinations are important to you in two ways. As a citizen, you want public jobs filled by employees who know how to do their work. As a job seeker, you want a fair chance to compete for that job on an equal footing with other candidates. The best-known means of accomplishing this two-fold goal is the competitive examination.

Exams are widely publicized throughout the nation. They may be administered for jobs in federal, state, city, municipal, town or village governments or agencies.

Any citizen may apply, with some limitations, such as the age or residence of applicants. Your experience and education may be reviewed to see whether you meet the requirements for the particular examination. When these requirements exist, they are reasonable and applied consistently to all applicants. Thus, a competitive examination may cause you some uneasiness now, but it is your privilege and safeguard.

C. HOW ARE CIVIL SERVICE EXAMS DEVELOPED?

Examinations are carefully written by trained technicians who are specialists in the field known as "psychological measurement," in consultation with recognized authorities in the field of work that the test will cover. These experts recommend the subject matter areas or skills to be tested; only those knowledges or skills important to your success on the job are included. The most reliable books and source materials available are used as references. Together, the experts and technicians judge the difficulty level of the questions.

Test technicians know how to phrase questions so that the problem is clearly stated. Their ethics do not permit "trick" or "catch" questions. Questions may have been tried out on sample groups, or subjected to statistical analysis, to determine their usefulness.

Written tests are often used in combination with performance tests, ratings of training and experience, and oral interviews. All of these measures combine to form the best-known means of finding the right person for the right job.

II. HOW TO PASS THE WRITTEN TEST

A. NATURE OF THE EXAMINATION

To prepare intelligently for civil service examinations, you should know how they differ from school examinations you have taken. In school you were assigned certain definite pages to read or subjects to cover. The examination questions were quite detailed and usually emphasized memory. Civil service exams, on the other hand, try to discover your present ability to perform the duties of a position, plus your potentiality to learn these duties. In other words, a civil service exam attempts to predict how successful you will be. Questions cover such a broad area that they cannot be as minute and detailed as school exam questions.

In the public service similar kinds of work, or positions, are grouped together in one "class." This process is known as *position-classification*. All the positions in a class are paid according to the salary range for that class. One class title covers all of these positions, and they are all tested by the same examination.

B. FOUR BASIC STEPS

1) Study the announcement

How, then, can you know what subjects to study? Our best answer is: "Learn as much as possible about the class of positions for which you've applied." The exam will test the knowledge, skills and abilities needed to do the work.

Your most valuable source of information about the position you want is the official exam announcement. This announcement lists the training and experience qualifications. Check these standards and apply only if you come reasonably close to meeting them.

The brief description of the position in the examination announcement offers some clues to the subjects which will be tested. Think about the job itself. Review the duties in your mind. Can you perform them, or are there some in which you are rusty? Fill in the blank spots in your preparation.

Many jurisdictions preview the written test in the exam announcement by including a section called "Knowledge and Abilities Required," "Scope of the Examination," or some similar heading. Here you will find out specifically what fields will be tested.

2) Review your own background

Once you learn in general what the position is all about, and what you need to know to do the work, ask yourself which subjects you already know fairly well and which need improvement. You may wonder whether to concentrate on improving your strong areas or on building some background in your fields of weakness. When the announcement has specified "some knowledge" or "considerable knowledge," or has used adjectives like "beginning principles of..." or "advanced ... methods," you can get a clue as to the number and difficulty of questions to be asked in any given field. More questions, and hence broader coverage, would be included for those subjects which are more important in the work. Now weigh your strengths and weaknesses against the job requirements and prepare accordingly.

3) Determine the level of the position

Another way to tell how intensively you should prepare is to understand the level of the job for which you are applying. Is it the entering level? In other words, is this the position in which beginners in a field of work are hired? Or is it an intermediate or advanced level? Sometimes this is indicated by such words as "Junior" or "Senior" in the class title. Other jurisdictions use Roman numerals to designate the level – Clerk I, Clerk II, for example. The word "Supervisor" sometimes appears in the title. If the level is not indicated by the title, check the description of duties. Will you be working under very close supervision, or will you have responsibility for independent decisions in this work?

4) Choose appropriate study materials

Now that you know the subjects to be examined and the relative amount of each subject to be covered, you can choose suitable study materials. For beginning level jobs, or even advanced ones, if you have a pronounced weakness in some aspect of your training, read a modern, standard textbook in that field. Be sure it is up to date and has general coverage. Such books are normally available at your library, and the librarian will be glad to help you locate one. For entry-level positions, questions of appropriate difficulty are chosen – neither highly advanced questions, nor those too simple. Such questions require careful thought but not advanced training.

If the position for which you are applying is technical or advanced, you will read more advanced, specialized material. If you are already familiar with the basic principles of your field, elementary textbooks would waste your time. Concentrate on advanced textbooks and technical periodicals. Think through the concepts and review difficult problems in your field.

These are all general sources. You can get more ideas on your own initiative, following these leads. For example, training manuals and publications of the government agency which employs workers in your field can be useful, particularly for technical and professional positions. A letter or visit to the government department involved may result in more specific study suggestions, and certainly will provide you with a more definite idea of the exact nature of the position you are seeking.

III. KINDS OF TESTS

Tests are used for purposes other than measuring knowledge and ability to perform specified duties. For some positions, it is equally important to test ability to make adjustments to new situations or to profit from training. In others, basic mental abilities not dependent on information are essential. Questions which test these things may not appear as pertinent to the duties of the position as those which test for knowledge and information. Yet they are often highly important parts of a fair examination. For very general questions, it is almost impossible to help you direct your study efforts. What we can do is to point out some of the more common of these general abilities needed in public service positions and describe some typical questions.

1) General information

Broad, general information has been found useful for predicting job success in some kinds of work. This is tested in a variety of ways, from vocabulary lists to questions about current events. Basic background in some field of work, such as sociology or economics, may be sampled in a group of questions. Often these are principles which have become familiar to most persons through exposure rather than through formal training. It is difficult to advise you how to study for these questions; being alert to the world around you is our best suggestion.

2) Verbal ability

An example of an ability needed in many positions is verbal or language ability. Verbal ability is, in brief, the ability to use and understand words. Vocabulary and grammar tests are typical measures of this ability. Reading comprehension or paragraph interpretation questions are common in many kinds of civil service tests. You are given a paragraph of written material and asked to find its central meaning.

3) Numerical ability

Number skills can be tested by the familiar arithmetic problem, by checking paired lists of numbers to see which are alike and which are different, or by interpreting charts and graphs. In the latter test, a graph may be printed in the test booklet which you are asked to use as the basis for answering questions.

4) Observation

A popular test for law-enforcement positions is the observation test. A picture is shown to you for several minutes, then taken away. Questions about the picture test your ability to observe both details and larger elements.

5) Following directions

In many positions in the public service, the employee must be able to carry out written instructions dependably and accurately. You may be given a chart with several columns, each column listing a variety of information. The questions require you to carry out directions involving the information given in the chart.

6) Skills and aptitudes

Performance tests effectively measure some manual skills and aptitudes. When the skill is one in which you are trained, such as typing or shorthand, you can practice. These tests are often very much like those given in business school or high school courses. For many of the other skills and aptitudes, however, no short-time preparation can be made. Skills and abilities natural to you or that you have developed throughout your lifetime are being tested.

Many of the general questions just described provide all the data needed to answer the questions and ask you to use your reasoning ability to find the answers. Your best preparation for these tests, as well as for tests of facts and ideas, is to be at your physical and mental best. You, no doubt, have your own methods of getting into an exam-taking mood and keeping "in shape." The next section lists some ideas on this subject.

IV. KINDS OF QUESTIONS

Only rarely is the "essay" question, which you answer in narrative form, used in civil service tests. Civil service tests are usually of the short-answer type. Full instructions for answering these questions will be given to you at the examination. But in case this is your first experience with short-answer questions and separate answer sheets, here is what you need to know:

1) Multiple-choice Questions

Most popular of the short-answer questions is the "multiple choice" or "best answer" question. It can be used, for example, to test for factual knowledge, ability to solve problems or judgment in meeting situations found at work.

A multiple-choice question is normally one of three types—

- It can begin with an incomplete statement followed by several possible endings. You are to find the one ending which *best* completes the statement, although some of the others may not be entirely wrong.
- It can also be a complete statement in the form of a question which is answered by choosing one of the statements listed.
- It can be in the form of a problem – again you select the best answer.

Here is an example of a multiple-choice question with a discussion which should give you some clues as to the method for choosing the right answer:

When an employee has a complaint about his assignment, the action which will *best* help him overcome his difficulty is to
A. discuss his difficulty with his coworkers
B. take the problem to the head of the organization
C. take the problem to the person who gave him the assignment
D. say nothing to anyone about his complaint

In answering this question, you should study each of the choices to find which is best. Consider choice "A" – Certainly an employee may discuss his complaint with fellow employees, but no change or improvement can result, and the complaint remains unresolved. Choice "B" is a poor choice since the head of the organization probably does not know what assignment you have been given, and taking your problem to him is known as "going over the head" of the supervisor. The supervisor, or person who made the assignment, is the person who can clarify it or correct any injustice. Choice "C" is, therefore, correct. To say nothing, as in choice "D," is unwise. Supervisors have and interest in knowing the problems employees are facing, and the employee is seeking a solution to his problem.

2) True/False Questions

The "true/false" or "right/wrong" form of question is sometimes used. Here a complete statement is given. Your job is to decide whether the statement is right or wrong.

SAMPLE: A roaming cell-phone call to a nearby city costs less than a non-roaming call to a distant city.

This statement is wrong, or false, since roaming calls are more expensive.
This is not a complete list of all possible question forms, although most of the others are variations of these common types. You will always get complete directions for

answering questions. Be sure you understand *how* to mark your answers – ask
questions until you do.

V. RECORDING YOUR ANSWERS

Computer terminals are used more and more today for many different kinds of
exams.

For an examination with very few applicants, you may be told to record your
answers in the test booklet itself. Separate answer sheets are much more common. If
this separate answer sheet is to be scored by machine – and this is often the case – it is
highly important that you mark your answers correctly in order to get credit.

An electronic scoring machine is often used in civil service offices because of the
speed with which papers can be scored. Machine-scored answer sheets must be
marked with a pencil, which will be given to you. This pencil has a high graphite content
which responds to the electronic scoring machine. As a matter of fact, stray dots may
register as answers, so do not let your pencil rest on the answer sheet while you are
pondering the correct answer. Also, if your pencil lead breaks or is otherwise defective,
ask for another.

Since the answer sheet will be dropped in a slot in the scoring machine, be
careful not to bend the corners or get the paper crumpled.

The answer sheet normally has five vertical columns of numbers, with 30
numbers to a column. These numbers correspond to the question numbers in your test
booklet. After each number, going across the page are four or five pairs of dotted lines.
These short dotted lines have small letters or numbers above them. The first two pairs
may also have a "T" or "F" above the letters. This indicates that the first two pairs only
are to be used if the questions are of the true-false type. If the questions are multiple
choice, disregard the "T" and "F" and pay attention only to the small letters or numbers.

Answer your questions in the manner of the sample that follows:

32. The largest city in the United States is
    A. Washington, D.C.
    B. New York City
    C. Chicago
    D. Detroit
    E. San Francisco

1) Choose the answer you think is best. (New York City is the largest, so "B" is
   correct.)
2) Find the row of dotted lines numbered the same as the question you are
   answering. (Find row number 32)
3) Find the pair of dotted lines corresponding to the answer. (Find the pair of
   lines under the mark "B.")
4) Make a solid black mark between the dotted lines.

VI. BEFORE THE TEST

Common sense will help you find procedures to follow to get ready for an
examination. Too many of us, however, overlook these sensible measures. Indeed,

nervousness and fatigue have been found to be the most serious reasons why applicants fail to do their best on civil service tests. Here is a list of reminders:

- Begin your preparation early – Don't wait until the last minute to go scurrying around for books and materials or to find out what the position is all about.
- Prepare continuously – An hour a night for a week is better than an all-night cram session. This has been definitely established. What is more, a night a week for a month will return better dividends than crowding your study into a shorter period of time.
- Locate the place of the exam – You have been sent a notice telling you when and where to report for the examination. If the location is in a different town or otherwise unfamiliar to you, it would be well to inquire the best route and learn something about the building.
- Relax the night before the test – Allow your mind to rest. Do not study at all that night. Plan some mild recreation or diversion; then go to bed early and get a good night's sleep.
- Get up early enough to make a leisurely trip to the place for the test – This way unforeseen events, traffic snarls, unfamiliar buildings, etc. will not upset you.
- Dress comfortably – A written test is not a fashion show. You will be known by number and not by name, so wear something comfortable.
- Leave excess paraphernalia at home – Shopping bags and odd bundles will get in your way. You need bring only the items mentioned in the official notice you received; usually everything you need is provided. Do not bring reference books to the exam. They will only confuse those last minutes and be taken away from you when in the test room.
- Arrive somewhat ahead of time – If because of transportation schedules you must get there very early, bring a newspaper or magazine to take your mind off yourself while waiting.
- Locate the examination room – When you have found the proper room, you will be directed to the seat or part of the room where you will sit. Sometimes you are given a sheet of instructions to read while you are waiting. Do not fill out any forms until you are told to do so; just read them and be prepared.
- Relax and prepare to listen to the instructions
- If you have any physical problem that may keep you from doing your best, be sure to tell the test administrator. If you are sick or in poor health, you really cannot do your best on the exam. You can come back and take the test some other time.

VII. AT THE TEST

The day of the test is here and you have the test booklet in your hand. The temptation to get going is very strong. Caution! There is more to success than knowing the right answers. You must know how to identify your papers and understand variations in the type of short-answer question used in this particular examination. Follow these suggestions for maximum results from your efforts:

1) Cooperate with the monitor

The test administrator has a duty to create a situation in which you can be as much at ease as possible. He will give instructions, tell you when to begin, check to see that you are marking your answer sheet correctly, and so on. He is not there to guard you, although he will see that your competitors do not take unfair advantage. He wants to help you do your best.

2) Listen to all instructions

Don't jump the gun! Wait until you understand all directions. In most civil service tests you get more time than you need to answer the questions. So don't be in a hurry. Read each word of instructions until you clearly understand the meaning. Study the examples, listen to all announcements and follow directions. Ask questions if you do not understand what to do.

3) Identify your papers

Civil service exams are usually identified by number only. You will be assigned a number; you must not put your name on your test papers. Be sure to copy your number correctly. Since more than one exam may be given, copy your exact examination title.

4) Plan your time

Unless you are told that a test is a "speed" or "rate of work" test, speed itself is usually not important. Time enough to answer all the questions will be provided, but this does not mean that you have all day. An overall time limit has been set. Divide the total time (in minutes) by the number of questions to determine the approximate time you have for each question.

5) Do not linger over difficult questions

If you come across a difficult question, mark it with a paper clip (useful to have along) and come back to it when you have been through the booklet. One caution if you do this – be sure to skip a number on your answer sheet as well. Check often to be sure that you have not lost your place and that you are marking in the row numbered the same as the question you are answering.

6) Read the questions

Be sure you know what the question asks! Many capable people are unsuccessful because they failed to *read* the questions correctly.

7) Answer all questions

Unless you have been instructed that a penalty will be deducted for incorrect answers, it is better to guess than to omit a question.

8) Speed tests

It is often better NOT to guess on speed tests. It has been found that on timed tests people are tempted to spend the last few seconds before time is called in marking answers at random – without even reading them – in the hope of picking up a few extra points. To discourage this practice, the instructions may warn you that your score will be "corrected" for guessing. That is, a penalty will be applied. The incorrect answers will be deducted from the correct ones, or some other penalty formula will be used.

9) Review your answers

If you finish before time is called, go back to the questions you guessed or omitted to give them further thought. Review other answers if you have time.

10) Return your test materials

If you are ready to leave before others have finished or time is called, take ALL your materials to the monitor and leave quietly. Never take any test material with you. The monitor can discover whose papers are not complete, and taking a test booklet may be grounds for disqualification.

VIII. EXAMINATION TECHNIQUES

1) Read the general instructions carefully. These are usually printed on the first page of the exam booklet. As a rule, these instructions refer to the timing of the examination; the fact that you should not start work until the signal and must stop work at a signal, etc. If there are any *special* instructions, such as a choice of questions to be answered, make sure that you note this instruction carefully.

2) When you are ready to start work on the examination, that is as soon as the signal has been given, read the instructions to each question booklet, underline any key words or phrases, such as *least, best, outline, describe* and the like. In this way you will tend to answer as requested rather than discover on reviewing your paper that you *listed without describing*, that you selected the *worst* choice rather than the *best* choice, etc.

3) If the examination is of the objective or multiple-choice type – that is, each question will also give a series of possible answers: A, B, C or D, and you are called upon to select the best answer and write the letter next to that answer on your answer paper – it is advisable to start answering each question in turn. There may be anywhere from 50 to 100 such questions in the three or four hours allotted and you can see how much time would be taken if you read through all the questions before beginning to answer any. Furthermore, if you come across a question or group of questions which you know would be difficult to answer, it would undoubtedly affect your handling of all the other questions.

4) If the examination is of the essay type and contains but a few questions, it is a moot point as to whether you should read all the questions before starting to answer any one. Of course, if you are given a choice – say five out of seven and the like – then it is essential to read all the questions so you can eliminate the two that are most difficult. If, however, you are asked to answer all the questions, there may be danger in trying to answer the easiest one first because you may find that you will spend too much time on it. The best technique is to answer the first question, then proceed to the second, etc.

5) Time your answers. Before the exam begins, write down the time it started, then add the time allowed for the examination and write down the time it must be completed, then divide the time available somewhat as follows:

- If 3-1/2 hours are allowed, that would be 210 minutes. If you have 80 objective-type questions, that would be an average of 2-1/2 minutes per question. Allow yourself no more than 2 minutes per question, or a total of 160 minutes, which will permit about 50 minutes to review.
- If for the time allotment of 210 minutes there are 7 essay questions to answer, that would average about 30 minutes a question. Give yourself only 25 minutes per question so that you have about 35 minutes to review.

6) The most important instruction is to *read each question* and make sure you know what is wanted. The second most important instruction is to *time yourself properly* so that you answer every question. The third most important instruction is to *answer every question*. Guess if you have to but include something for each question. Remember that you will receive no credit for a blank and will probably receive some credit if you write something in answer to an essay question. If you guess a letter – say "B" for a multiple-choice question – you may have guessed right. If you leave a blank as an answer to a multiple-choice question, the examiners may respect your feelings but it will not add a point to your score. Some exams may penalize you for wrong answers, so in such cases *only*, you may not want to guess unless you have some basis for your answer.

7) Suggestions
   a. Objective-type questions
      1. Examine the question booklet for proper sequence of pages and questions
      2. Read all instructions carefully
      3. Skip any question which seems too difficult; return to it after all other questions have been answered
      4. Apportion your time properly; do not spend too much time on any single question or group of questions
      5. Note and underline key words – *all, most, fewest, least, best, worst, same, opposite,* etc.
      6. Pay particular attention to negatives
      7. Note unusual option, e.g., unduly long, short, complex, different or similar in content to the body of the question
      8. Observe the use of "hedging" words – *probably, may, most likely,* etc.
      9. Make sure that your answer is put next to the same number as the question
      10. Do not second-guess unless you have good reason to believe the second answer is definitely more correct
      11. Cross out original answer if you decide another answer is more accurate; do not erase until you are ready to hand your paper in
      12. Answer all questions; guess unless instructed otherwise
      13. Leave time for review

   b. Essay questions
      1. Read each question carefully
      2. Determine exactly what is wanted. Underline key words or phrases.
      3. Decide on outline or paragraph answer

4. Include many different points and elements unless asked to develop any one or two points or elements
5. Show impartiality by giving pros and cons unless directed to select one side only
6. Make and write down any assumptions you find necessary to answer the questions
7. Watch your English, grammar, punctuation and choice of words
8. Time your answers; don't crowd material

8) Answering the essay question

Most essay questions can be answered by framing the specific response around several key words or ideas. Here are a few such key words or ideas:

M's: manpower, materials, methods, money, management
P's: purpose, program, policy, plan, procedure, practice, problems, pitfalls, personnel, public relations

   a. Six basic steps in handling problems:
      1. Preliminary plan and background development
      2. Collect information, data and facts
      3. Analyze and interpret information, data and facts
      4. Analyze and develop solutions as well as make recommendations
      5. Prepare report and sell recommendations
      6. Install recommendations and follow up effectiveness

   b. Pitfalls to avoid
      1. *Taking things for granted* – A statement of the situation does not necessarily imply that each of the elements is necessarily true; for example, a complaint may be invalid and biased so that all that can be taken for granted is that a complaint has been registered
      2. *Considering only one side of a situation* – Wherever possible, indicate several alternatives and then point out the reasons you selected the best one
      3. *Failing to indicate follow up* – Whenever your answer indicates action on your part, make certain that you will take proper follow-up action to see how successful your recommendations, procedures or actions turn out to be
      4. *Taking too long in answering any single question* – Remember to time your answers properly

IX. AFTER THE TEST

Scoring procedures differ in detail among civil service jurisdictions although the general principles are the same. Whether the papers are hand-scored or graded by machine we have described, they are nearly always graded by number. That is, the person who marks the paper knows only the number – never the name – of the applicant. Not until all the papers have been graded will they be matched with names. If other tests, such as training and experience or oral interview ratings have been given, scores will be combined. Different parts of the examination usually have different weights. For example, the written test might count 60 percent of the final grade, and a rating of training and experience 40 percent. In many jurisdictions, veterans will have a certain number of points added to their grades.

After the final grade has been determined, the names are placed in grade order and an eligible list is established. There are various methods for resolving ties between those who get the same final grade – probably the most common is to place first the name of the person whose application was received first. Job offers are made from the eligible list in the order the names appear on it. You will be notified of your grade and your rank as soon as all these computations have been made. This will be done as rapidly as possible.

People who are found to meet the requirements in the announcement are called "eligibles." Their names are put on a list of eligible candidates. An eligible's chances of getting a job depend on how high he stands on this list and how fast agencies are filling jobs from the list.

When a job is to be filled from a list of eligibles, the agency asks for the names of people on the list of eligibles for that job. When the civil service commission receives this request, it sends to the agency the names of the three people highest on this list. Or, if the job to be filled has specialized requirements, the office sends the agency the names of the top three persons who meet these requirements from the general list.

The appointing officer makes a choice from among the three people whose names were sent to him. If the selected person accepts the appointment, the names of the others are put back on the list to be considered for future openings.

That is the rule in hiring from all kinds of eligible lists, whether they are for typist, carpenter, chemist, or something else. For every vacancy, the appointing officer has his choice of any one of the top three eligibles on the list. This explains why the person whose name is on top of the list sometimes does not get an appointment when some of the persons lower on the list do. If the appointing officer chooses the second or third eligible, the No. 1 eligible does not get a job at once, but stays on the list until he is appointed or the list is terminated.

X. HOW TO PASS THE INTERVIEW TEST

The examination for which you applied requires an oral interview test. You have already taken the written test and you are now being called for the interview test – the final part of the formal examination.

You may think that it is not possible to prepare for an interview test and that there are no procedures to follow during an interview. Our purpose is to point out some things you can do in advance that will help you and some good rules to follow and pitfalls to avoid while you are being interviewed.

What is an interview supposed to test?
The written examination is designed to test the technical knowledge and competence of the candidate; the oral is designed to evaluate intangible qualities, not readily measured otherwise, and to establish a list showing the relative fitness of each candidate – as measured against his competitors – for the position sought. Scoring is not on the basis of "right" and "wrong," but on a sliding scale of values ranging from "not passable" to "outstanding." As a matter of fact, it is possible to achieve a relatively low score without a single "incorrect" answer because of evident weakness in the qualities being measured.

Occasionally, an examination may consist entirely of an oral test – either an individual or a group oral. In such cases, information is sought concerning the technical knowledges and abilities of the candidate, since there has been no written examination for this purpose. More commonly, however, an oral test is used to supplement a written examination.

Who conducts interviews?

The composition of oral boards varies among different jurisdictions. In nearly all, a representative of the personnel department serves as chairman. One of the members of the board may be a representative of the department in which the candidate would work. In some cases, "outside experts" are used, and, frequently, a businessman or some other representative of the general public is asked to serve. Labor and management or other special groups may be represented. The aim is to secure the services of experts in the appropriate field.

However the board is composed, it is a good idea (and not at all improper or unethical) to ascertain in advance of the interview who the members are and what groups they represent. When you are introduced to them, you will have some idea of their backgrounds and interests, and at least you will not stutter and stammer over their names.

What should be done before the interview?

While knowledge about the board members is useful and takes some of the surprise element out of the interview, there is other preparation which is more substantive. It *is* possible to prepare for an oral interview – in several ways:

1) Keep a copy of your application and review it carefully before the interview

This may be the only document before the oral board, and the starting point of the interview. Know what education and experience you have listed there, and the sequence and dates of all of it. Sometimes the board will ask you to review the highlights of your experience for them; you should not have to hem and haw doing it.

2) Study the class specification and the examination announcement

Usually, the oral board has one or both of these to guide them. The qualities, characteristics or knowledges required by the position sought are stated in these documents. They offer valuable clues as to the nature of the oral interview. For example, if the job involves supervisory responsibilities, the announcement will usually indicate that knowledge of modern supervisory methods and the qualifications of the candidate as a supervisor will be tested. If so, you can expect such questions, frequently in the form of a hypothetical situation which you are expected to solve. NEVER go into an oral without knowledge of the duties and responsibilities of the job you seek.

3) Think through each qualification required

Try to visualize the kind of questions you would ask if you were a board member. How well could you answer them? Try especially to appraise your own knowledge and background in each area, *measured against the job sought*, and identify any areas in which you are weak. Be critical and realistic – do not flatter yourself.

4) Do some general reading in areas in which you feel you may be weak

For example, if the job involves supervision and your past experience has NOT, some general reading in supervisory methods and practices, particularly in the field of human relations, might be useful. Do NOT study agency procedures or detailed manuals. The oral board will be testing your understanding and capacity, not your memory.

5) Get a good night's sleep and watch your general health and mental attitude

You will want a clear head at the interview. Take care of a cold or any other minor ailment, and of course, no hangovers.

What should be done on the day of the interview?

Now comes the day of the interview itself. Give yourself plenty of time to get there. Plan to arrive somewhat ahead of the scheduled time, particularly if your appointment is in the fore part of the day. If a previous candidate fails to appear, the board might be ready for you a bit early. By early afternoon an oral board is almost invariably behind schedule if there are many candidates, and you may have to wait. Take along a book or magazine to read, or your application to review, but leave any extraneous material in the waiting room when you go in for your interview. In any event, relax and compose yourself.

The matter of dress is important. The board is forming impressions about you – from your experience, your manners, your attitude, and your appearance. Give your personal appearance careful attention. Dress your best, but not your flashiest. Choose conservative, appropriate clothing, and be sure it is immaculate. This is a business interview, and your appearance should indicate that you regard it as such. Besides, being well groomed and properly dressed will help boost your confidence.

Sooner or later, someone will call your name and escort you into the interview room. *This is it.* From here on you are on your own. It is too late for any more preparation. But remember, you asked for this opportunity to prove your fitness, and you are here because your request was granted.

What happens when you go in?

The usual sequence of events will be as follows: The clerk (who is often the board stenographer) will introduce you to the chairman of the oral board, who will introduce you to the other members of the board. Acknowledge the introductions before you sit down. Do not be surprised if you find a microphone facing you or a stenotypist sitting by. Oral interviews are usually recorded in the event of an appeal or other review.

Usually the chairman of the board will open the interview by reviewing the highlights of your education and work experience from your application – primarily for the benefit of the other members of the board, as well as to get the material into the record. Do not interrupt or comment unless there is an error or significant misinterpretation; if that is the case, do not hesitate. But do not quibble about insignificant matters. Also, he will usually ask you some question about your education, experience or your present job – partly to get you to start talking and to establish the interviewing "rapport." He may start the actual questioning, or turn it over to one of the other members. Frequently, each member undertakes the questioning on a particular area, one in which he is perhaps most competent, so you can expect each member to participate in the examination. Because time is limited, you may also expect some rather abrupt switches in the direction the questioning takes, so do not be upset by it. Normally, a board member will not pursue a single line of questioning unless he discovers a particular strength or weakness.

After each member has participated, the chairman will usually ask whether any member has any further questions, then will ask you if you have anything you wish to add. Unless you are expecting this question, it may floor you. Worse, it may start you off on an extended, extemporaneous speech. The board is not usually seeking more information. The question is principally to offer you a last opportunity to present further qualifications or to indicate that you have nothing to add. So, if you feel that a significant qualification or characteristic has been overlooked, it is proper to point it out in a sentence or so. Do not compliment the board on the thoroughness of their examination – they have been sketchy, and you know it. If you wish, merely say, "No thank you, I have nothing further to add." This is a point where you can "talk yourself out" of a good impression or fail to present an important bit of information. Remember, *you close the interview yourself.*

The chairman will then say, "That is all, Mr. _____, thank you." Do not be startled; the interview is over, and quicker than you think. Thank him, gather your belongings and take your leave. Save your sigh of relief for the other side of the door.

How to put your best foot forward

Throughout this entire process, you may feel that the board individually and collectively is trying to pierce your defenses, seek out your hidden weaknesses and embarrass and confuse you. Actually, this is not true. They are obliged to make an appraisal of your qualifications for the job you are seeking, and they want to see you in your best light. Remember, they must interview all candidates and a non-cooperative candidate may become a failure in spite of their best efforts to bring out his qualifications. Here are 15 suggestions that will help you:

1) Be natural – Keep your attitude confident, not cocky

If you are not confident that you can do the job, do not expect the board to be. Do not apologize for your weaknesses, try to bring out your strong points. The board is interested in a positive, not negative, presentation. Cockiness will antagonize any board member and make him wonder if you are covering up a weakness by a false show of strength.

2) Get comfortable, but don't lounge or sprawl

Sit erectly but not stiffly. A careless posture may lead the board to conclude that you are careless in other things, or at least that you are not impressed by the importance of the occasion. Either conclusion is natural, even if incorrect. Do not fuss with your clothing, a pencil or an ashtray. Your hands may occasionally be useful to emphasize a point; do not let them become a point of distraction.

3) Do not wisecrack or make small talk

This is a serious situation, and your attitude should show that you consider it as such. Further, the time of the board is limited – they do not want to waste it, and neither should you.

4) Do not exaggerate your experience or abilities

In the first place, from information in the application or other interviews and sources, the board may know more about you than you think. Secondly, you probably will not get away with it. An experienced board is rather adept at spotting such a situation, so do not take the chance.

5) If you know a board member, do not make a point of it, yet do not hide it

Certainly you are not fooling him, and probably not the other members of the board. Do not try to take advantage of your acquaintanceship – it will probably do you little good.

6) Do not dominate the interview

Let the board do that. They will give you the clues – do not assume that you have to do all the talking. Realize that the board has a number of questions to ask you, and do not try to take up all the interview time by showing off your extensive knowledge of the answer to the first one.

7) Be attentive

You only have 20 minutes or so, and you should keep your attention at its sharpest throughout. When a member is addressing a problem or question to you, give him your undivided attention. Address your reply principally to him, but do not exclude the other board members.

8) Do not interrupt

A board member may be stating a problem for you to analyze. He will ask you a question when the time comes. Let him state the problem, and wait for the question.

9) Make sure you understand the question

Do not try to answer until you are sure what the question is. If it is not clear, restate it in your own words or ask the board member to clarify it for you. However, do not haggle about minor elements.

10) Reply promptly but not hastily

A common entry on oral board rating sheets is "candidate responded readily," or "candidate hesitated in replies." Respond as promptly and quickly as you can, but do not jump to a hasty, ill-considered answer.

11) Do not be peremptory in your answers

A brief answer is proper – but do not fire your answer back. That is a losing game from your point of view. The board member can probably ask questions much faster than you can answer them.

12) Do not try to create the answer you think the board member wants

He is interested in what kind of mind you have and how it works – not in playing games. Furthermore, he can usually spot this practice and will actually grade you down on it.

13) Do not switch sides in your reply merely to agree with a board member

Frequently, a member will take a contrary position merely to draw you out and to see if you are willing and able to defend your point of view. Do not start a debate, yet do not surrender a good position. If a position is worth taking, it is worth defending.

14) Do not be afraid to admit an error in judgment if you are shown to be wrong

The board knows that you are forced to reply without any opportunity for careful consideration. Your answer may be demonstrably wrong. If so, admit it and get on with the interview.

15) Do not dwell at length on your present job

The opening question may relate to your present assignment. Answer the question but do not go into an extended discussion. You are being examined for a *new* job, not your present one. As a matter of fact, try to phrase ALL your answers in terms of the job for which you are being examined.

Basis of Rating

Probably you will forget most of these "do's" and "don'ts" when you walk into the oral interview room. Even remembering them all will not ensure you a passing grade. Perhaps you did not have the qualifications in the first place. But remembering them will help you to put your best foot forward, without treading on the toes of the board members.

Rumor and popular opinion to the contrary notwithstanding, an oral board wants you to make the best appearance possible. They know you are under pressure – but they also want to see how you respond to it as a guide to what your reaction would be under the pressures of the job you seek. They will be influenced by the degree of poise you display, the personal traits you show and the manner in which you respond.

ABOUT THIS BOOK

This book contains tests divided into Examination Sections. Go through each test, answering every question in the margin. At the end of each test look at the answer key and check your answers. On the ones you got wrong, look at the right answer choice and learn. Do not fill in the answers first. Do not memorize the questions and answers, but understand the answer and principles involved. On your test, the questions will likely be different from the samples. Questions are changed and new ones added. If you understand these past questions you should have success with any changes that arise. Tests may consist of several types of questions. We have additional books on each subject should more study be advisable or necessary for you. Finally, the more you study, the better prepared you will be. This book is intended to be the last thing you study before you walk into the examination room. Prior study of relevant texts is also recommended. NLC publishes some of these in our Fundamental Series. Knowledge and good sense are important factors in passing your exam. Good luck also helps. So now study this Passbook, absorb the material contained within and take that knowledge into the examination. Then do your best to pass that exam.

———

EXAMINATION SECTION

EXAMINATION SECTION
TEST 1

DIRECTIONS: Each question or incomplete statement is followed by several suggested answers or completions. Select the one that BEST answers the question or completes the statement. *PRINT THE LETTER OF THE CORRECT ANSWER IN THE SPACE AT THE RIGHT.*

1. If you open a personal letter by mistake, the one of the following actions which it would generall be BEST for   u to take is to   1.____

   A.   ignore your error, attach the envelope to the letter, and distribute in the usual man-
        ner
   B.   personally give the addressee the letter without any explanation
   C.   place the letter inside the envelope, indicate under your initials that it was opened
        in error, and give to the addressee
   D.   reseal the envelope or place the contents in another envelope and pass on to
        addressee

2. If you receive a telephone call regarding a matter which your office does not handle, you should FIRST   2.____

   A.   give the caller the telephone number of the proper office so that he can dial again
   B.   offer to transfer the caller to the proper office
   C.   suggest that the caller re-dial since he probably dialed incorrectly
   D.   tell the caller he has reached the wrong office and then hang up

3. When you answer the telephone, the MOST important reason for identifying yourself and your organization is to   3.____

   A.   give the caller time to collect his or her thoughts
   B.   impress the caller with your courtesy
   C.   inform the caller that he or she has reached the right number
   D.   set a business-like tone at the beginning of the conversatio

4. The one of the following cases in which you would NOT place a special notation in the left margin of a letter that you have typed is when   4.____

   A.   one of the copies is intended for someone other than the addressee of the
        letter
   B.   you enclose a flyer with the letter
   C.   you sign your superior's name to the letter at his or her request
   D.   the letter refers to something being sent under separate cover

5. Suppose that you accidentally cut a letter or enclosure as you are opening an envelope with a paper knife.   5.____
    The one of the following that you should do FIRST is to

   A.   determine whether the document is important
   B.   clip or staple the pieces together and process as usual
   C.   mend the cut document with transparent tape
   D.   notify the sender that the communication was damaged and request another copy

6. It is generally advisable to leave at least six inches of working space in a file drawer.   6.____
This procedure is MOST useful in

    A. decreasing the number of filing errors
    B. facilitating the sorting of documents and folders
    C. maintaining a regular program of removing inactive records
    D. preventing folders and papers from being torn

7. Of the following, the MOST important reason to sort large volumes of documents before   7.____
filing is that sorting

    A. decreases the need for cross-referencing
    B. eliminates the need to keep the files up to date
    C. prevents overcrowding of the file drawers
    D. saves time and energy in filing

8. When typing a preliminary draft of a report, the one of the following which you should   8.____
generally NOT do is to

    A. erase typing errors and deletions rather than x-ing them out
    B. leave plenty of room at the top, bottom and sides of each page
    C. make only the number of copies that you are asked to make
    D. type double or triple space

9. The BEST way for a receptionist to deal with a situation in which she must leave her desk   9.____
for a long time is to

    A. ask someone to take her place while she is away
    B. leave a note or sign on her desk which indicates the time she will return
    C. take a chance that no one will arrive while she is gone and leave her desk unat-
tended
    D. tell a co-worker to ask any visitors that arrive to wait until she returns

10. Suppose that two individuals come up to your desk at the same time. One of them asks   10.____
you for the location of the nearest public phone. After you answer the question, you turn
to the second person who asks you the same question. The one of the following actions
which it would be BEST for you to take in this situation is to

    A. ignore the second person since he obviously overheard your first answer
    B. point out that you just answered the same question and quickly repeat the informa-
tion
    C. politely repeat the information to the second individual
    D. tell the second person to follow the first to the public telephone

11. Suppose that you are newly assigned to a large office in your department. You believe   11.____
that a certain change in office routine would be desirable.
Of the following, the BEST reason for suggesting this modification to your supervisor is
that

    A. even good supervisors are sometimes reluctant to institute innovations
    B. your suggestion may result in the saving of considerable time and money
    C. major changes in office routine are easier to make in small offices than in large
offices
    D. a new employee will usually be able to think of new ways of doing his work

12. When typing names or titles on a roll of folder labels, the one of the following which it is   12.____
    MOST important to do is to type the caption

    A. as it appears on the papers to be placed in the folder
    B. in capital letters
    C. in exact indexing or filing order
    D. so that it appears near the bottom of the folder tab when the label is attached

Questions 13-17.

DIRECTIONS: Questions 13 through 17 consist of the names of students who have applied
               for a certain college program and are to be classified according to the criteria
               described below.

The following table gives pertinent data for 6 different applicants with regard to:
Grade averages, which are expressed on a scale running from
        0 (low) to 4 (high);
Scores on qualifying test, which run from 200 (low) to 800 (high); Related work experience,
which is expressed in number of months; Personal references, which are rated from 1 (low)
to 5 (high).

Applicant	Grade Average	Test Score	Work Experience	Reference
Jones	2.2	620	24	3
Perez	3.5	650	0	5
Lowitz	3.2	420	2	4
Uncker	2.1	710	15	2
Farrow	2.8	560	0	3
Shapiro	3.0	560	12	4

An administrative assistant is in charge of the initial screening process for the program.
This process requires classifying applicants into the following four groups:

    A. SUPERIOR CANDIDATES. Unless the personal reference rating is lower than 3, all
        applicants with grade averages of 3.0 or higher and test scores of 600 or higher are
        classified as superior candidates.
    B. GOOD CANDIDATES. Unless the personal reference rating is lower than 3, all
        applicants with one of the following combinations of grade averages and test
        scores are classified as good candidates: (1) grade average of 2.5 to 2.9 and test
        score of 600 or higher; (2) grade average of 3.0 or higher and test score of 550 to
        599.
    C. POSSIBLE CANDIDATES. Applicants with one of the following combinations of
        qualifications are classified as possible candidates: (1) grade average of 2.5 to 2.9
        and test score of 550 to 599 and a personal reference rating of 3 or higher; (2)
        grade average of 2.0 to 2.4 and test score of 500 or higher and at least 21 months'
        work experience and a personal reference rating of 3 or higher; (3) a combination
        of grade average and test score that would otherwise qualify as *superior* or *good*
        but a personal reference score lower than 3.
    D. REJECTED CANDIDATES. Applicants who do not fall in any of the above groups
        are to be rejected.

EXAMPLE
Jones' grade average of 2.2 does not meet the standard for either a superior candidate (grade average must be 3.0 or higher) or a good candidate (grade average must be 2.5 to 2.9). Grade average of 2.2 does not qualify Jones as a possible candidate if Jones has a test score of 500 or higher, at least 21 months' work experience, and a personal reference rating of 3 or higher. Since Jones has a test score of 620, 24 months' work experience, and a reference rating of 3, Jones is a possible candidate. The answer is C.

Answer Questions 13 through 17 as explained above, indicating for each whether the applicant should be classified as a

A. superior candidate
B. good candidate
C. possible candidate
D. rejected candidate

13. Perez   13._____
14. Lowitz   14._____
15. Uncker   15._____
16. Farrow   16._____
17. Shapiro   17._____

18. An *attention* line is used in correspondence to   18._____

A. indicate to the person receiving the correspondence that it contains an enclosure
B. direct correspondence addressed to an organization to a particular individual within the organization
C. greet the recipient of the correspondence
D. highlight the main concern of the correspondence

19. The MOST important reason for a person in charge of a petty cash fund to obtain receipts for payments is that this practice would tend to   19._____

A. decrease robberies by delivery personnel
B. eliminate the need to keep a record of petty cash expenditures
C. prove that the fund has been used properly
D. provide a record of the need for cash in the daily operations of the office

20. You should generally replenish a petty cash fund   20._____

A. at regularly established intervals
B. each time you withdraw a sum of more than $2.00
C. when the amount of cash gets below a certain specified amount
D. when the fund is completely empty

Questions 21-32.

DIRECTIONS: In Questions 21 through 32, choose the lettered word which means MOST NEARLY the same as the italicized word in the sentence.

21. The aims of the students and the aims of the faculty often *coincide*.   21._____

A. agree
B. are ignored
C. conflict
D. are misinterpreted

22. The secretary of the sociology department was responsible for setting up an index of *relevant* magazine articles.   22._____

A. applicable
B. controversial
C. miscellaneous
D. recent

23. One of the secretary's duties consisted of sorting and filing *facsimiles* of student term papers.   23.____

    A. bibliographical listings   B. exact copies
    C. summaries   D. supporting documentation

24. *Stringent* requirements for advanced physics courses often result in small class sizes.   24.____

    A. lengthy   B. remarkable   C. rigid   D. vague

25. The professor explained that the report was too *verbose* to be submitted.   25.____

    A. brief   B. specific   C. general   D. wordy

26. The faculty meeting *pre-empted* the conference room in the Dean's office.   26.____

    A. appropriated   B. emptied
    C. filled   D. reserved

27. The professor's credentials became a subject of *controversy*.   27.____

    A. annoyance   B. debate   C. envy   D. review

28. The professor developed a different central theme during every *semester*   28.____

    A. bi-annual period of instruction
    B. orientation period
    C. slide demonstration
    D. weekly lecture series

29. The college offered a variety of *seminars* to upperclassmen.   29.____

    A. reading courses with no formal supervision
    B. study courses for small groups of students engaged
    C. in research under a teacher
    D. guidance conferences with grade advisors
    E. work experiences in different occupational fields

30. The Dean pointed out that the *focus* of the study was not clear.   30.____

    A. end   B. objective   C. follow-up   D. location

31. The faculty of the anthropology department agreed that the departmental program was *deficient*.   31.____

    A. excellent   B. inadequate   C. demanding   D. sufficien

32. The secretary was asked to type a rough draft of a college course *syllabus*.   32.____

    A. directory of departments and services
    B. examination schedule
    C. outline of a course of study
    D. rules and regulations

Questions 33-40.

DIRECTIONS: Each of the questions numbered 33 through 40 consists of three sets of names and name codes. In each question, the two names and name codes on the same line are supposed to be exactly the same.

Look carefully at each set of names and codes and mark your answer
A. if there are mistakes in all three sets
B. if there are mistakes in two of the sets
C. if there is a mistake in only one set
D. if there are no mistakes in any of the sets

SAMPLE QUESTION

The following sample question is given to help you understand the procedure:

Macabe, John N.- V 53162 Macade, John N.-　V 53162
Howard, Joan S.- J 24791 Howard, Joan S. -　J 24791
Ware, Susan B. -　A 45068 Ware, Susan B. -　A45968

In the above sample question, the names and name codes of the first set are not exactly the same because of the spelling of the last name (Macabe - Macade). The names and name codes of the second set are exactly the same.

The names and name codes of the third set are not exactly the same because the two name codes are different (A 45068 - A 45968). Since there are mistakes in only two of the sets, the answer to the sample question is B.

33.	Powell, Michael C.	-	78537 F	Powell, Michael C.	-	78537 F	33._____
	Martinez, Pablo J.	-	24435 P	Martinez, Pablo J.	-	24435 P	
	MacBane, Eliot M.	-	98674 E	MacBane, Eliot M.	-	98674 E	

34.	Fitz-Kramer Machines Inc.	-	259090	Fitz-Kramer Machines Inc.	-	259090	34._____
	Marvel Cleaning Service	-	482657	Marvel Cleaning Service	-	482657	
	Donato, Carl G.	-	637418	Danato, Carl G.	-	687418	

35.	Martin Davison Trading Corp.	-	43108 T	Martin Davidson Trading Corp.	-	43108 T	35._____
	Cotwald Lighting Fixtures	-	70056 L	Cotwald Lighting Fixtures	-	76065 L	
	R. Crawford Plumbers	-	23157 G	R. Crawford Plumbers	-	23157 C	

36.	Fraiman Engineering Corp.	-	M4773	Friaman Engineering Corp.	-	M4773	36._____
	Neuman, Walter B.	-	N7745	Neumen, Walter B.	-	N7745	
	Pierce, Eric M.	-	W6304	Pierce, Eric M.	-	W6304	

37.	Constable, Eugene	-	B 64837	Comstable, Eugene	-	B 64837	37._____
	Derrick, Paul	-	H 27119	Derrik, Paul	-	H 27119	
	Heller, Karen	-	S 49606	Heller, Karen	-	S 46906	

38.	Hernando Delivery Service Co.			Hernando Delivery Service Co.			38._____
		-	D 7456		-	D 7456	
	Barettz Electrical Supplies	-	N 5392	Barettz Electrical Supplies	-	N 5392	
	Tanner, Abraham	-	M 4798	Tanner, Abraham	-	M 4798	

39.	Kalin Associates	-	R 38641	Kaline Associates	-	R 38641	39._____
	Sealey, Robert E.	-	P 63533	Sealey, Robert E.	-	P 63553	
	Scalsi Office Furniture	-	R 36742	Scalsi Office Furniture	-	R 36742	

40.	Janowsky, Philip M.	-	742213	Janowsky, Philip M.	-	742213	40._____
	Hansen, Thomas H.	-	934816	Hanson, Thomas H.	-	934816	
	L. Lester and Son Inc.	-	294568	L. Lester and Son Inc.	-	294568	

KEY (CORRECT ANSWERS)

1.	C	11.	B	21.	A	31.	B
2.	B	12.	C	22.	A	32.	C
3.	C	13.	A	23.	B	33.	D
4.	C	14.	D	24.	C	34.	C
5.	C	15.	D	25.	D	35.	A
6.	D	16.	C	26.	A	36.	B
7.	D	17.	B	27.	B	37.	A
8.	A	18.	B	28.	A	38.	D
9.	A	19.	C	29.	B	39.	B
10.	C	20.	C	30.	B	40.	C

TEST 2

DIRECTIONS: Each question or incomplete statement is followed by several suggested answers or completions. Select the one that BEST answers the question or completes the statement. *PRINT THE LETTER OF THE CORRECT ANSWER IN THE SPACE AT THE RIGHT.*

1. When you determine the methods of emphasis you will use in typing the titles, headings, and subheadings of a report, the one of the following which it is MOST important to keep in mind is that

    A. all headings of the same rank should be typed in the same way
    B. all headings should be typed in the single style which is most pleasing to the eye
    C. headings should not take up more than one-third of the page width
    D. only one method should be used for all headings, whatever their rank

1.____

2. After checking several times, you are unable to locate a student record in its proper file drawer. The file drawer in question is used constantly by many members of the staff. In this situation, the NEXT step you should take in locating the missing record is to

    A. ask another worker to look through the file drawer
    B. determine if there is another copy of the record filed in a different place
    C. find out if the record has been removed by another staff member
    D. wait a day or two and see if the record turns up

2.____

3. It is MOST important that an enclosure which is to be mailed with a letter should be put in an envelope so that

    A. any printing on the enclosure will not be visible through the address side of the envelope
    B. it is obvious that there is an enclosure inside the envelope
    C. the enclosure takes up less space than the letter
    D. the person who opens the envelope will put out both the letter and the enclosure

3.____

4. Suppose that one of the student aides with whom you work suggests a change in the filing procedure. He is sure the change will result in increased rates of filing among the other employees.
The one of the following which you should do FIRST is to

    A. ask him to demonstrate his method in order to determine if he files more quickly than the other employees
    B. ask your supervisor if you may make a change in the filing procedure
    C. ignore the aide's suggestion since he is not a filing expert
    D. tell him to show his method to the other employees and to encourage them to use it

4.____

5. When opening mail by hand, the one of the following methods which would generally be BEST to use is to

    A. cut off one end of the envelope
    B. cut off the top of the envelope
    C. place the envelope face down on your desk and pull the flap of the envelope back
    D. place the envelope face down on your desk and run a sharp flat instrument under the flap

5.____

6. Suppose that the chairman of a program in a senior college where you work has asked   6._____
   you for the entire file folder on a particular student in the program.
   Since he tells you that he may have the folder out for some time, it would generally be
   BEST for you to

   A. make a copy of each document in the folder, prepare a new folder, and place it in
      the file
   B. place an out folder in the file
   C. place a cross-reference card in the file
   D. place a slip of paper in the file indicating why the folder was removed

7. The one of the following ways in which inter-office memoranda differ from long formal   7._____
   reports is that they GENERALLY

   A. are written as if the reader is familiar with the vocabulary and technical background
      of the writer
   B. do not have a *subject line* which describes the major topic covered in the text
   C. include a listing of reference materials which support the memo writer's conclu-
      sions
   D. require that a letter of transmittal be attached

Questions 8-15.

DIRECTIONS: Each Question 8 through 15 consists of four names. For each question,
              choose the one of the four names that should be LAST if the four names were
              arranged in alphabetical order in accordance with the RULES FOR ALPHA-
              BETICAL FILING given below. Read these rules carefully. Then, for each
              question, indicate in the numbered space at the right the letter before the
              name that should be LAST in alphabetical order.

RULES FOR ALPHABETICAL FILING

Names of Individuals.

1. *The names of individuals are filed in strict alphabetical order, first according to the last
   name, then according to first name or initial, and finally according to middle name or initial. For example: George Allen comes before Edward Bell, and Leonard P. Reston
   comes before Lucille B. Reston.*

2. *When last names are the same, for example, A. Green and Agnes Green, the one with
   the initial comes before the one with the name written out when the first initials are identical.*

3. *When first and last names are alike, the name without a middle initial comes before the
   one with a middle name or initial. For example: John Doe comes before both John A.
   Doe and John Alan Doe.*

4. *When first and last names are the same, the name with a middle initial comes before the
   one with a middle name beginning with the same initial. For example: Jack R. Herts
   comes before Jack Richard Hertz.*

5. Prefixes such as De, 0', Mac, Mc, and Van are filed as written and are treated as part of the names they come before. For example: Robert 0 'Dea is filed before David Olsen.

6. Abbreviated names are treated as if they were spelled out. For example: Chas. is filed as Charles, and Thos. is filed as Thomas.

7. Titles and designations such as Dr., Mr., and Prof, are disregarded in filing.

Names of Business Organizations.

1. The names of business organizations are filed according to the order in which each word in the name appears. When an organization name bears the name of a person, it is filed according to the rules for filing names of people as given above. For example: William Smith Service Co. comes before Television Distributors, Inc.

2. When the following words are part of a business name, they are disregarded: the, of, and.

3. When there are numbers in a name, they are treated as if they were spelled out. For example: 10th Street Bootery is filed as Tenth Street Bootery.

Names of Government Offices

Bureaus, boards, offices, and departments of the city government are filed under the name of the chief governing body. For example: Bureau of the Budget would be filed as if written Budget (Bureau of the) .

SAMPLE QUESTION:

A.	Jane Earl	(2)
B.	James A. Earle	(4)
C.	James Earl	(1)
D.	J. Earle	(3)

The numbers in parentheses show the proper alphabetical order in which these names should be filed. Since the name that should be filed LAST is James A. Earle, the answer to the Sample Question is B.

8. A. Corral, Dr. Robert　　　　　　　　　　　　　　　　　　　8.____
    B. Carrale, Prof. Robert
    C. Corren, R.
    D. Corret, Ron

9. A. Rivera, Ilena　　　　　　　　　　　　　　　　　　　　　9.____
    B. Riviera, Ilene
    C. Rivere, I.
    D. Riviera Ice-Cream Co.

10. A. VonHogel, George　　　　　　　　　　　　　　　　　　10.____
    B. Volper, Gary
    C. Vonner, G.
    D. Van Pefel, Gregory

11. A. David Kallish Stationery Co.   11._____
     B. Emerson Microfilm Company
     C. David Kalder Industrial Engineers Associated
     D. 5th Avenue Office Furniture Co.

12. A. Bennet, C.   12._____
     B. Benett, Chuck
     C. Bennet, Chas.
     D. Bennett, Charles

13. A. The Board of Higher Education   13._____
     A. National Education Commission
     B. Eakin, Hugh
     C. Nathan, Ellen

14. A. McCloud, I.   14._____
     B. MacGowen, Ian
     C. McGowen, Arthur
     D. Macale, Sean

15. A. Devine, Sarah   15._____
     B. Devine, S.
     C. Devine, Sara H.
     D. Devin, Sarah

Questions 16-21.

DIRECTIONS: Answer Questions 16 through 21 SOLELY on the basis of the following paragraphs.

A folder is made of a sheet of heavy paper (manila, kraft, press-board, or red rope stock) that has been folded once so that the back is about one-half inch higher than the front. Folders are larger than the papers they contain in order to protect them. Two standard folder sizes are "letter size" for papers that are 8 1/2" x 11" and "legal cap" for papers that are 8 1/2" x 13".

Folders are cut across the top in two ways: so that the back is straight (straight-cut), or so that the back has a tab that projects above the top of the folder. Such tabs bear captions that identify the contents of each folder. Tabs vary in width and position. The tabs of a set of folders that are "one-half cut" are half the width of the folder, and have only two positions.

"One-third cut" folders have three positions, each tab occupying a third of the width of the folder. Another standard tabbing is "one-fifth cut," which has five positions. There are also folders with "two-fifths cut, " with the tabs in the third and fourth, or fourth and fifth, positions.

16. Of the following, the BEST title for the above passage is   16._____

A. Filing Folders
C. The Uses of the Folder
B. Standard Folder Sizes
D. The Use of Tabs

17. According to the above passage, one of the standard folder sizes is called   17.____

    A. kraft cut
    C. one-half cut
    B. legal cap
    D. straight-cut

18. According to the above passage, tabs are GENERALLY placed along the _____ of the   18.____
folder.

    A. back
    C. left side
    B. front
    D. right side

19. According to the above passage, a tab is GENERALLY used to   19.____

    A. distinguish between standard folder sizes
    B. identify the contents of a folder
    C. increase the size of the folder
    D. protect the papers within the folder

20. According to the above passage, a folder that is two-fifths cut has _____ tabs.   20.____

    A. no   B. two   C. three   D. five

21. According to the above passage, one reason for making folders larger than the papers   21.____
they contain is that

    A. only a certain size folder can be made from heavy paper
    B. they will protect the papers
    C. they will aid in setting up a tab system
    D. the back of the folder must be higher than the front

Questions 22-30.

DIRECTIONS: Answer Questions 22 through 30 SOLELY on the basis of the following paragraphs.

The City University of New York traces its origins to 1847, when the Free Academy,
which later became City College, was founded as the first tuition-free municipal college. City
and Hunter Colleges were placed under the direction of the Board of Higher Education in
1926, and Brooklyn and Queens Colleges were subsequently added to the system of municipal colleges. In 1955, Staten Island Community College, the first of the two-year colleges
sponsored by the Board of Higher Education under the program of the State University of flew
York, joined the system.

In 1961, the four senior colleges and three community colleges then under the jurisdiction of the Board of Higher Education became the City University of New York, and a University Graduate Division was organized to offer programs leading to the Ph.D. Since then, the
university has undergone even more rapid growth. Today it consists of nine senior colleges,
an upper division college which admits students at the junior level, eight community colleges,
a graduate division, and an affiliated medical center.

In the summer of 1969, the Board of Higher Education resolved that the time had come to commit the resources of the university to meeting an urgent social need -- unrestricted access to higher education for all youths of the City. Determined to prevent the waste of human potential represented by the thousands of high school graduates whose limited educational opportunities left them unable to meet existing admission standards, the Board moved to adopt a policy of Open Admissions. It was their judgment that the best way of determining whether a potential student can benefit from college work is to admit him to college, provide him with the learning assistance he needs, and then evaluate his performance.

Beginning with the class of June 1970, every New York City resident who receives a high school diploma from a public or private high school is guaranteed a place in one of the colleges of City University.

22. Of the following, the BEST title for the above passage is   22.____

    A. A Brief History of the City University
    B. High Schools and the City University
    C. The Components of the University
    D. Tuition-Free Colleges

23. According to the above passage, the one of the following colleges of the City University   23.____
which was ORIGINALLY called the Free Academy was _____ College.

    A. Brooklyn   B. City   C. Hunter   D. Queens

24. According to the above passage, the system of municipal colleges became the City University of New York in   24.____

    A. 1926   B. 1955   C. 1961   D. 1969

25. According to the above passage, Staten Island Community College came under the jurisdiction of the Board of Higher Education   25.____

    A. 6 years after a Graduate Division was organized
    B. 8 years before the adoption of the Open Admissions Policy
    C. 29 years after Brooklyn and Queens Colleges
    D. 29 years after City and Hunter Colleges

26. According to the above passage, the Staten Island Community College is a(n)   26.____

    A. graduate division center   B. senior college
    C. two-year college   D. upper division college

27. According to the above passage, the TOTAL number of colleges, divisions, and affiliated branches of the City University is   27.____

    A. 18   B. 19   C. 20   D. 21

28. According to the above passage, the open admissions policy is designed to determine whether a potential student will benefit from college by PRIMARILY   28.____

    A. discouraging competition for placement in the City University among high school students
    B. evaluating his performance after entry into college

C. lowering admission standards
D. providing learning assistance before entry into college

29. According to the above passage, the FIRST class to be affected by the open admissions   29.____
     policy was the

   A. high school class which graduated in January 1970
   B. City University class which graduated in June 1970
   C. high school class which graduated in June 1970
   D. City University class which graduated in January 1970

30. According to the above passage, one of the reasons that the Board of Higher Education   30.____
     initiated the policy of open admissions was to

   A. enable high school graduates with a background of limited educational opportuni-
       ties to enter college
   B. expand the growth of the City University so as to increase the number and variety
       of degrees offered
   C. provide a social resource to the qualified youth of the City
   D. revise admission standards to meet the needs of the City

Questions 31-37.

DIRECTIONS: Answer Questions 31 through 37 SOLELY on the basis of the table below
             referring to agency Part-time employees.

Deductions

Emp. No.	Name	Exempt.	Gross Earnings	Fed. With. Tax	FICA	Grp. Ins	Hosp.	Bonds	Total Deductions	Net Earnings
123	Anderson, Paul	1	72.50	7.90	3.64	.85	.95		13.34	59.16
209	Greene, Henry	4	85.00	4.00	2.52	.85	.95		8.32	76.68
27	Kowalski, Anna	2	158.33	17.30	8.03	.97	1.10		27.50	130.83
174	Rodriguez, Marie	1	85.00	7.45	2.52	.80	.95		11.72	73.28
362	Rosen, Carl	2	112.28	12.40	5.48	.80	.95		19.63	92.65
198	Sung, Wang Y.	3	95.00	6.00	3.77	.93	1.05	2.00	13.75	81.25
53	Tomasso, Francis	4	190.81	18.60	8.56	1.12	1.20	3.00	32.48	158.33
	Total		798.92	73.65	34.62	6.32	7.15	5.00	126.74	672.18

31. According to the above chart, the sum of the total deductions is APPROXIMATELY what   31.____
     percent of the total gross earnings?

   A. 6.3%   B. 9.3%   C. 15.8%   D. 18.6%

32. According to the above chart, the sum of the net earnings of two of the employees is MOST NEARLY the same as the gross earnings of the employee named

    A. Anna Kowalski   B. Carl Rosen
    C. Henry Greene   D. Wang Y. Sung

32.____

33. According to the above chart, the AVERAGE amount deducted for Federal withholding tax of all employees with gross earnings over $100 is

    A. $5.55   B. $6.33   C. $16.10   D. $17.95

33.____

34. According to the above chart, the AVERAGE net earnings for all employees with net earnings below $100 is *approximately*

    A. $67.34   B. $76.60   C. $84.38   D. $96.20

34.____

35. According to the above chart, the employee who has the HIGHEST percent of his or her gross earnings deducted is

    A. Paul Anderson   B. Henry Greene
    C. Anna Kowalski   D. Carl Rosen

35.____

36. According to the above chart, the number of employees whose Federal withholding tax is GREATER than 10% of their gross earnings is

    A. 2   B. 3   C. 4   D. 5

36.____

37. According to the above chart, the net earnings of one employee are equal to the gross earnings of another employee.
The TWO employees about whom this statement can be made are:

    A. Marie Rodriguez and Carl Rosen
    B. Paul Anderson and Henry Greene
    C. Henry Greene and Marie Rodriguez
    D. Anna Kowalski and Francis Tomasso

37.____

38. You are preparing a package of six books to mail to a professor who is on sabbatical. They weigh, respectively, 1 pound 11 ounces, 1 pound 6 ounces, 2 pounds 1 ounce, 2 pounds 2 ounces, 1 pound 7 ounces, and 1 pound 8 ounces. The packaging material weighs 6 ounces.
The TOTAL weight of the package will be _____ pounds _____ ounces.

    A. 10; 3   B. 10; 9   C. 11; 5   D. 12; 5

38.____

39. Part-time students are charged $35.00 per credit for courses at a particular college. In addition, they must pay a $12.00 student activity fee if they take six credits or more and a $7.00 lab fee for each laboratory course.
If a person takes one 3-credit course and one 4-credit course and his 4-credit course is a laboratory course, the TOTAL cost to him will be

    A. $252.00   B. $264.00   C. $271.00   D. $276.00

39.____

40. The graduating class of a certain community college consisted of 378 majors in secretarial science, 265 majors in engineering science, 57 majors in nursing, 513 majors in accounting, and 865 majors in liberal arts. The percent of students who major in liberal arts at this college was MOST NEARLY   40.____

    A. 24.0%   B. 41.6%   C. 52.3%   D. 71.6%

KEY (CORRECT ANSWERS)

1.	A	11.	A	21.	B	31.	C
2.	C	12.	D	22.	A	32.	A
3.	D	13.	B	23.	B	33.	C
4.	A	14.	C	24.	C	34.	B
5.	D	15.	A	25.	B	35.	A
6.	B	16.	A	26.	C	36.	B
7.	A	17.	B	27.	C	37.	D
8.	D	18.	A	28.	B	38.	B
9.	B	19.	B	29.	C	39.	B
10.	C	20.	B	30.	A	40.	B

16

EXAMINATION SECTION
TEST 1

DIRECTIONS: Each question or incomplete statement is followed by several suggested answers or completions. Select the one that BEST answers the question or completes the statement. *PRINT THE LETTER OF THE CORRECT ANSWER IN THE SPACE AT THE RIGHT.*

1. Assume that a few co-workers meet near your desk and talk about personal matters during working hours. Lately, this practice has interfered with your work.
In order to stop this practice, the BEST action for you to take FIRST is to

    A. ask your supervisor to put a stop to the co-workers' meeting near your desk
    B. discontinue any friendship with this group
    C. ask your co-workers not to meet near your desk
    D. request that your desk be moved to another location

1.____

2. In order to maintain office coverage during working hours, your supervisor has scheduled your lunch hour from 1 P.M. to 2 P.M. and your co-worker's lunch hour from 12 P.M. to 1 P.M. Lately, your co-worker has been returning late from lunch each day. As a result, you don't get a full hour since you must return to the office by 2 P.M.
Of the following, the BEST action for you to take FIRST is to

    A. explain to your co-worker in a courteous manner that his lateness is interfering with your right to a full hour for lunch
    B. tell your co-worker that his lateness must stop or you will report him to your supervisor
    C. report your co-worker's lateness to your supervisor
    D. leave at 1 P.M. for lunch, whether your co-worker has returned or not

2.____

3. Assume that, as an office worker, one of your jobs is to open mail sent to your unit, read the mail for content, and send the mail to the appropriate person to handle. You accidentally open and begin to read a letter marked *personal* addressed to a co-worker.
Of the following, the BEST action for you to take is to

    A. report to your supervisor that your co-worker is receiving personal mail at the office
    B. destroy the letter so that your co-worker does not know you saw it
    C. reseal the letter and place it on the co-worker's desk without saying anything
    D. bring the letter to your co-worker and explain that you opened it by accident

3.____

4. Suppose that in evaluating your work, your supervisor gives you an overall good rating, but states that you sometimes turn in work with careless errors.
The BEST action for you to take would be to

    A. ask a co-worker who is good at details to proofread your work
    B. take time to do a careful job, paying more attention to detail
    C. continue working as usual since occasional errors are to be expected
    D. ask your supervisor if she would mind correcting your errors

4.____

5. Assume that you are taking a telephone message for a co-worker who is not in the office at the time.
Of the following, the LEAST important item to write on the message is the

    A. length of the call   B. name of the caller
    C. time of the call   D. telephone number of the caller

5.____

Questions 6-13.

DIRECTIONS: Questions 6 through 13 each consist of a sentence which may or may not be an example of good English. The underlined parts of each sentence may be correct or incorrect. Examine each sentence, considering grammar, punctuation, spelling, and capitalization. If the English usage in the underlined parts of the sentence given is better than any of the changes in the underlined words suggested in Options B, C, or D, choose Option A. If the changes in the underlined words suggested in Options B, C, or D would make the sentence correct, choose the correct option. Do not choose an option that will change the meaning of the sentence.

6.   This <u>Fall</u>, the office will be closed on <u>Columbus Day, October</u> 9th.   6._____

    A.   Correct as is
    B.   fall...Columbus Day, October
    C.   Fall...columbus day, October
    D.   fall...Columbus Day, october

7.   This manual <u>discribes the duties performed</u> by an Office Aide.   7._____

    A.   Correct as is
    B.   describe the duties performed
    C.   discribe the duties performed
    D.   describes the duties performed

8.   There <u>weren't no</u> paper in the supply closet.   8._____

    A.   Correct as is   B.   weren't any
    C.   wasn't any   D.   wasn't no

9.   The new employees left <u>there</u> office to attend a meeting.   9._____

    A.   Correct as is   B.   they're
    C.   their   D.   thier

10.   The office worker started working at <u>8:30 a.m.</u>   10._____

    A.   Correct as is   B.   8:30 a.m.
    C.   8;30 a,m.   D.   8:30 am

11.   The <u>alphabet, or A to Z sequence</u> are the basis of most filing systems.   11._____

    A.   Correct as is
    B.   alphabet, or A to Z sequence, is
    C.   alphabet, or A to Z sequence are
    D.   alphabet, or A too Z sequence, is

12.   <u>Those</u> file cabinets are five <u>feet</u> tall.   12._____

    A.   Correct as is   B.   Them...feet
    C.   Those...foot   D.   Them...foot

13. The Office Aide checked the <u>register and finding</u> the date of the meeting.   13.____

    A. Correct as is   B. regaster and finding
    C. register and found   D. regaster and found

Questions 14-21.

DIRECTIONS: Each of Questions 14 through 21 has two lists of numbers. Each list contains three sets of numbers. Check each of the three sets in the list on the right to see if they are the same as the corresponding set in the list on the left. Mark your answers:

    A. If none of the sets in the right list are the same as those in the left list
    B. if only one of the sets in the right list are the same as those in the left list
    C. if only two of the sets in the right list are the same as those in the left list
    D. if all three sets in the right list are the same as those in the left list

14. 7354183476   7354983476   14.____
     4474747744   4474747774
     57914302311   57914302311

15. 7143592185   7143892185   15.____
     8344517699   8344518699
     9178531263   9178531263

16. 2572114731   257214731   16.____
     8806835476   8806835476
     8255831246   8255831246

17. 331476853821   331476858621   17.____
     6976658532996   6976655832996
     3766042113715   3766042113745

18. 8806663315   8806663315   18.____
     74477138449   74477138449
     211756663666   211756663666

19. 990006966996   99000696996   19.____
     53022219743   53022219843
     4171171117717   4171171177717

20. 24400222433004   24400222433004   20.____
     5300030055000355   5300030055500355
     20000075532002022   20000075532002022

21. 611166640660001116   61116664066001116   21.____
     7111300117001100733   7111300117001100733
     26666446664476518   26666446664476518

Questions 22-25.

DIRECTIONS: Each of Questions 22 through 25 has two lists of names and addresses. Each list contains three sets of names and addresses. Check each of the three sets in the list on the right to see if they are the same as the corresponding set in the list on the left. Mark your answers:

A. if none of the sets in the right list are the same as those in the left list
B. if only one of the sets in the right list is the same as those in the left list
C. if only two of the sets in the right list are the same as those in the left list
D. if all three sets in the right list are the same as those in the left list

22. Mary T. Berlinger
    2351 Hampton St.
    Monsey, N.Y. 20117

    Eduardo Benes
    473 Kingston Avenue
    Central Islip, N.Y. 11734

    Alan Carrington Fuchs
    17 Gnarled Hollow Road
    Los Angeles, CA 91635

    Mary T. Berlinger
    2351 Hampton St.
    Monsey, N.Y. 20117

    Eduardo Benes
    473 Kingston Avenue
    Central Islip, N.Y. 11734

    Alan Carrington Fuchs
    17 Gnarled Hollow Road
    Los Angeles, CA 91685

22.____

23. David John Jacobson
    178 35 St. Apt. 4C
    New York, N.Y. 00927

    Ann-Marie Calonella
    7243 South Ridge Blvd.
    Bakersfield, CA 96714

    Pauline M. Thompson
    872 Linden Ave.
    Houston, Texas 70321

    David John Jacobson
    178 53 St. Apt. 4C
    New York, N.Y. 00927

    Ann-Marie Calonella
    7243 South Ridge Blvd.
    Bakersfield, CA 96714

    Pauline M. Thomson
    872 Linden Ave.
    Houston, Texas 70321

23.____

24. Chester LeRoy Masterton
    152 Lacy Rd.
    Kankakee, Ill. 54532

    William Maloney
    S. LaCrosse Pla.
    Wausau, Wisconsin 52146

    Cynthia V. Barnes
    16 Pines Rd.
    Greenpoint, Miss. 20376

    Chester LeRoy Masterson
    152 Lacy Rd.
    Kankakee, Ill. 54532

    William Maloney
    S. LaCross Pla.
    Wausau, Wisconsin 52146

    Cynthia V. Barnes
    16 Pines Rd.
    Greenpoint, Miss. 20376

24.____

25. Marcel Jean Frontenac
      6 Burton On The Water
      Calender, Me. 01471

      J. Scott Marsden
      174 S. Tipton St.
      Cleveland, Ohio

      Lawrence T. Haney
      171 McDonough St.
      Decatur, Ga. 31304

Marcel Jean Frontenac
6 Burton On The Water
Calender, Me. 01471

J. Scott Marsden
174 Tipton St.
Cleveland, Ohio

Lawrence T. Haney
171 McDonough St.
Decatur, Ga. 31304

25.____

KEY (CORRECT ANSWERS)

1.	C		11.	B
2.	A		12.	A
3.	D		13.	C
4.	B		14.	B
5.	A		15.	B
6.	A		16.	C
7.	D		17.	A
8.	C		18.	D
9.	C		19.	A
10.	B		20.	C

21. C
22. C
23. B
24. B
25. C

TEST 2

DIRECTIONS: Each question or incomplete statement is followed by several suggested answers or completions. Select the one that BEST answers the question or completes the statement. *PRINT THE LETTER OF THE CORRECT ANSWER IN THE SPACE AT THE RIGHT.*

Questions 1-6.

DIRECTIONS: Questions 1 through 6 are to be answered SOLELY on the basis of the information contained in the following passage.

Duplicating is the process of making a number of identical copies of letters, documents, etc. from an original. Some duplicating processes make copies directly from the original document. Other duplicating processes require the preparation of a special master, and copies are then made from the master. Four of the most common duplicating processes are stencil, fluid, offset, and xerox.

In the stencil process, the typewriter is used to cut the words into a master called a stencil. Drawings, charts, or graphs can be cut into the stencil using a stylus. As many as 3,500 good-quality copies can be reproduced from one stencil. Various grades of finished paper from inexpensive mimeograph to expensive bond can be used.

The fluid process is a good method of copying from 50 to 125 good-quality copies from a master, which is prepared with a special dye. The master is placed on the duplicator, and special paper with a hard finish is moistened and then passed through the duplicator. Some of the dye on the master is dissolved, creating an impression on the paper. The impression becomes lighter as more copies are made; and once the dye on the master is used up, a new master must be made.

The offset process is the most adaptable office duplicating process because this process can be used for making a few copies or many copies. Masters can be made on paper or plastic for a few hundred copies, or on metal plates for as many as 75,000 copies. By using a special technique called photo-offset, charts, photographs, illustrations, or graphs can be reproduced on the master plate. The offset process is capable of producing large quantities of fine, top-quality copies on all types of finished paper.

The xerox process reproduces an exact duplicate from an original. It is the fastest duplicating method because the original material is placed directly on the duplicator, eliminating the need to make a special master. Any kind of paper can be used. The xerox process is the most expensive duplicating process; however, it is the best method of reproducing small quantities of good-quality copies of reports, letters, official documents, memos, or contracts.

1. Of the following, the MOST efficient method of reproducing 5,000 copies of a graph is   1.____

    A. stencil   B. fluid   C. offset   D. xerox

2. The offset process is the MOST adaptable office duplicating process because   2.____

    A. it is the quickest duplicating method
    B. it is the least expensive duplicating method
    C. it can produce a small number or large number of copies
    D. a softer master can be used over and over again

3. Which one of the following duplicating processes uses moistened paper? 3.____

   A. Stencil B. Fluid C. Offset D. Xerox

4. The fluid process would be the BEST process to use for reproducing 4.____

   A. five copies of a school transcript
   B. fifty copies of a memo
   C. five hundred copies of a form letter
   D. five thousand copies of a chart

5. Which one of the following duplicating processes does NOT require a special master? 5.____

   A. Fluid B. Xerox C. Offset D. Stencil

6. Xerox is NOT used for all duplicating jobs because 6.____

   A. it produces poor-quality copies
   B. the process is too expensive
   C. preparing the master is too time-consuming
   D. it cannot produce written reports

7. Assume a city agency has 775 office workers. 7.____
   If 2 out of 25 office workers were absent on a particular day, how many office workers reported to work on that day?

   A. 713 B. 744 C. 750 D. 773

Questions 8-11.

DIRECTIONS: In Questions 8 through 11, select the choice that is CLOSEST in meaning to the underlined word.

SAMPLE: This division reviews the fiscal reports of the agency.
In this sentence, the word fiscal means MOST NEARLY
A. financial B. critical C. basic D. personnel

The correct answer is A, financial, because financial is closest to fiscal.

8. A central file eliminates the need to retain duplicate material. 8.____
   The word retain means MOST NEARLY

   A. keep B. change C. locate D. process

9. Filing is a routine office task. 9.____
   Routine means MOST NEARLY

   A. proper B. regular C. simple D. difficult

10. Sometimes a word, phrase, or sentence must be deleted to correct an error. 10.____
    Deleted means MOST NEARLY

    A. removed B. added C. expanded D. improved

11. Your supervisor will <u>evaluate</u> your work.   11.____
    <u>Evaluate</u> means MOST NEARLY

    A. judge   B. list   C. assign   D. explain

Questions 12-19.

DIRECTIONS: The code table below shows 10 letters with matching numbers. For each
               Question 12 through 19, there are three sets of letters. Each set of letters is
               followed by a set of numbers which may or may not match their correct letter
               according to the code table. For each question, check all three sets of letters
               and numbers and mark your answer:
               A. if no pairs are correctly matched
               B. if only one pair is correctly matched
               C. if only two pairs are correctly matched
               D. if all three pairs are correctly matched

<u>CODE TABLE</u>

T	M	V	D	S	P	R	G	B	H
1	2	3	4	5	6	7	8	9	0

<u>Sample Question:</u>   TMVDSP - 123456
                          RGBHTM - 789011
                          DSPRGB - 256789

In the sample question above, the first set of numbers correctly matches its set of letters. But
the second and third pairs contain mistakes. In the second pair, M is incorrectly matched with
number 1. According to the code table, letter M should be correctly matched with number 2. In
the third pair, the letter D is incorrectly matched with number 2. According to the code table, letter D should be correctly matched with number 4. Since only one of the pairs is correctly
matched, the answer to this sample question is B.

12. RSBMRM - 759262   12.____
     GDSRVH - 845730
     VDBRTM - 349713

13. TGVSDR - 183247   13.____
     SMHRDP - 520647
     TRMHSR - 172057

14. DSPRGM - 456782   14.____
     MVDBHT - 234902
     HPMDBT - 062491

15. BVPTRD - 936184   15.____
     GDPHMB - 807029
     GMRHMV - 827032

16. MGVRSH - 283750   16.____
     TRDMBS - 174295
     SPRMGV - 567283

24

17. SGBSDM   -   489542
    MGHPTM   -   290612
    MPBMHT   -   269301

17.____

18. TDPBHM   -   146902
    VPBMRS   -   369275
    GDMBHM   -   842902

18.____

19. MVPTBV   -   236194
    PDRTMB   -   647128
    BGTMSM   -   981232

19.____

Questions 20-25.

DIRECTIONS: In each of Questions 20 through 25, the names of four people are given. For each question, choose as your answer the one of the four names given which should be filed FIRST according to the usual system of alphabetical filing of names, as described in the following paragraph.

In filing names, you must start with the last name. Names are filed in order of the first letter of the last name, then the second letter, etc. Therefore, BAILY would be filed before BROWN, which would be filed before COLT. A name with fewer letters of the same type comes first; i.e., Smith before Smithe. If the last names are the same, the names are filed alphabetically by the first name. If the first name is an initial, a name with an initial would come before a first name that starts with the same letter as the initial. Therefore, I. BROWN would come before IRA BROWN. Finally, if both last name and first name are the same, the name would be filed alphabetically by the middle name, one again an initial coming before a middle name which starts with the same letter as the initial. If there is no middle name at all, the name would come before those with middle initials or names.

Sample Question: A. Lester Daniels
                         B. William Dancer
                         C. Nathan Danzig
                         D. Dan Lester

The last names beginning with D are filed before the last name beginning with L. Since DANIELS, DANCER, and DANZIG all begin with the same three letters, you must look at the fourth letter of the last name to determine which name should be filed first. C comes before I or Z in the alphabet, so DANCER is filed before DANIELS or DANZIG. Therefore, the answer to the above sample question is B.

20.   A. Scott Biala   B. Mary Byala
      C. Martin Baylor   D. Francis Bauer

20.____

21.   A. Howard J. Black   B. Howard Black
      C. J. Howard Black   D. John H. Black

21.____

22.   A. Theodora Garth Kingston   B. Theadore Barth Kingston
      C. Thomas Kingston   D. Thomas T. Kingston

22.____

23.   A. Paulette Mary Huerta   B. Paul M. Huerta
      C. Paulette L. Huerta   D. Peter A. Huerta

23.____

24. A. Martha Hunt Morgan   B. Martin Hunt Morgan   24.____
     C. Mary H. Morgan   D. Martine H. Morgan

25. A. James T. Meerschaum   B. James M. Mershum   25.____
     C. James F. Mearshaum   D. James N. Meshum

KEY (CORRECT ANSWERS)

1.	C	11.	A
2.	C	12.	B
3.	B	13.	B
4.	B	14.	C
5.	B	15.	A
6.	B	16.	D
7.	A	17.	A
8.	A	18.	D
9.	B	19.	A
10.	A	20.	D

21.	B
22.	B
23.	B
24.	A
25.	C

TEST 3

DIRECTIONS: Each question or incomplete statement is followed by several suggested answers or completions. Select the one that BEST answers the question or completes the statement. *PRINT THE LETTER OF THE CORRECT ANSWER IN THE SPACE AT THE RIGHT.*

1. Which one of the following statements about proper telephone usage is NOT always correct?
   When answering the telephone, you should

   A. know whom you are speaking to
   B. give the caller your undivided attention
   C. identify yourself to the caller
   D. obtain the information the caller wishes before you do your other work

   1._____

2. Assume that, as a member of a worker's safety committee in your agency, you are responsible for encouraging other employees to follow correct safety practices. While you are working on your regular assignment, you observe an employee violating a safety rule.
   Of the following, the BEST action for you to take FIRST is to

   A. speak to the employee about safety practices and order him to stop violating the safety rule
   B. speak to the employee about safety practices and point out the safety rule he is violating
   C. bring the matter up in the next committee meeting
   D. report this violation of the safety rule to the employee's supervisor

   2._____

3. Assume that you have been temporarily assigned by your supervisor to do a job which you do not want to do. The BEST action for you to take is to

   A. discuss the job with your supervisor, explaining why you do not want to do it
   B. discuss the job with your supervisor and tell her that you will not do it
   C. ask a co-worker to take your place on this job
   D. do some other job that you like; your supervisor may give the job you do not like to someone else

   3._____

4. Assume that you keep the confidential personnel files of employees in your unit. A friend asks you to obtain some information from the file of one of your co-workers.
   The BEST action to take is to _____ to your friend.

   A. ask the co-worker if you can give the information
   B. ask your supervisor if you can give the information
   C. give the information
   D. refuse to give the information

   4._____

Questions 5-8.

DIRECTIONS: Questions 5 through 8 are to be answered SOLELY on the basis of the information contained in the following passage.

City government is committed to providing a safe and healthy work environment for all city employees. An effective agency safety program reduces accidents by educating employees about the types of careless acts which can cause accidents. Even in an office, accidents can happen. If each employee is aware of possible safety hazards, the number of accidents on the job can be reduced.

Careless use of office equipment can cause accidents and injuries. For example, file cabinet drawers which are filled with papers can be so heavy that the entire cabinet could tip over from the weight of one open drawer.

The bottom drawers of desks and file cabinets should never be left open since employees could easily trip over open drawers and injure themselves.

When reaching for objects on a high shelf, an employee should use a strong, sturdy object such as a step stool to stand on. Makeshift platforms made out of books, papers, or boxes can easily collapse. Even chairs can slide out from under foot, causing serious injury.

Even at an employee's desk, safety hazards can occur. Frayed or cut wires should be repaired or replaced immediately. Computers which are not firmly anchored to the desk or table could fall, causing injury.

Smoking is one of the major causes of fires in the office. A lighted match or improperly extinguished cigarette thrown into a wastebasket filled with paper could cause a major fire with possible loss of life. Where smoking is permitted, ashtrays should be used. Smoking is particularly dangerous in offices where flammable chemicals are used.

5. The goal of an effective safety program is to   5.____

    A. reduce office accidents
    B. stop employees from smoking on the job
    C. encourage employees to continue their education
    D. eliminate high shelves in offices

6. Desks and file cabinets can become safety hazards when   6.____

    A. their drawers are left open
    B. they are used as wastebaskets
    C. they are makeshift
    D. they are not anchored securely to the floor

7. Smoking is especially hazardous when it occurs   7.____

    A. near exposed wires
    B. in a crowded office
    C. in an area where flammable chemicals are used
    D. where books and papers are stored

8. Accidents are likely to occur when   8.____

    A. employees' desks are cluttered with books and papers
    B. employees are not aware of safety hazards
    C. employees close desk drawers
    D. step stools are used to reach high objects

9. Assume that part of your job as a worker in the accounting division of a city agency is to answer the telephone. When you first answer the telephone, it is LEAST important to tell the caller

    A. your title   B. your name
    C. the name of your unit   D. the name of your agency

10. Assume that you are assigned to work as a receptionist, and your duties are to answer phones, greet visitors, and do other general office work. You are busy with a routine job when several visitors approach your desk.
The BEST action to take is to

    A. ask the visitors to have a seat and assist them after your work is completed
    B. tell the visitors that you are busy and they should return at a more convenient time
    C. stop working long enough to assist the visitors
    D. continue working and wait for the visitors to ask you for assistance

11. Assume that your supervisor has chosen you to take a special course during working hours to learn a new payroll procedure. Although you know that you were chosen because of your good work record, a co-worker, who feels that he should have been chosen, has been telling everyone in your unit that the choice was unfair.
Of the following, the BEST way to handle this situation FIRST is to

    A. suggest to the co-worker that everything in life is unfair
    B. contact your union representative in case your co-worker presents a formal grievance
    C. tell your supervisor about your co-worker's complaints and let her handle the situation
    D. tell the co-worker that you were chosen because of your superior work record

12. Assume that while you are working on an assignment which must be completed quickly, a supervisor from another unit asks you to obtain information for her.
Of the following, the BEST way to respond to her request is to

    A. tell her to return in an hour since you are busy
    B. give her the names of some people in her own unit who could help her
    C. tell her you are busy and refer her to a co-worker
    D. tell her that you are busy and ask her if she could wait until you finish your assignment

13. A co-worker in your unit is often off from work because of illness. Your supervisor assigns the co-worker's work to you when she is not there. Lately, doing her work has interfered with your own job.
The BEST action for you to take FIRST is to

    A. discuss the problem with your supervisor
    B. complete your own work before starting your co-worker's work
    C. ask other workers in your unit to assist you
    D. work late in order to get the jobs done

14. During the month of June, 40,587 people attended a city-owned swimming pool. In July, 13,014 more people attended the swimming pool than the number that had attended in June. In August, 39,655 people attended the swimming pool.
The TOTAL number of people who attended the swimming pool during the months of June, July, and August was

    A. 80,242   B. 93,256   C. 133,843   D. 210,382

14.____

Questions 15-22.

DIRECTIONS: Questions 15 through 22 test how well you understand what you read. It will be necessary for you to read carefully because your answers to these questions must be based ONLY on the information in the following paragraphs.

The telephone directory is made up of two books. The first book consists of the introductory section and the alphabetical listing of names section. The second book is the classified directory (also known as the yellow pages). Many people who are familiar with one book do not realize how useful the other can be. The efficient office worker should become familiar with both books in order to make the best use of this important source of information.

The introductory section gives general instructions for finding numbers in the alphabetical listing and classified directory. This section also explains how to use the telephone company's many services, including the operator and information services, gives examples of charges for local and long-distance calls, and lists area codes for the entire country. In addition, this section provides a useful postal zip code map.

The alphabetical listing of names section lists the names, addresses, and telephone numbers of subscribers in an area. Guide names, or *telltales,* are on the top corner of each page. These guide names indicate the first and last name to be found on that page. *Telltales* help locate any particular name quickly. A cross-reference spelling is also given to help locate names which are spelled several different ways. City, state, and federal government agencies are listed under the major government heading. For example, an agency of the federal government would be listed under *United States Government.*

The classified directory, or yellow pages, is a separate book. In this section are advertising services, public transportation line maps, shopping guides, and listings of businesses arranged by the type of product or services they offer. This book is most useful when looking for the name or phone number of a business when all that is known is the type of product offered and the address, or when trying to locate a particular type of business in an area. Businesses listed in the classified directory can usually be found in the alphabetical listing of names section. When the name of the business is known, you will find the address or phone number more quickly in the alphabetical listing of names section.

15. The introductory section provides

    A. shopping guides   B. government listings
    C. business listings   D. information services

15.____

16. Advertising services would be found in the

    A. introductory section   B. alphabetical listing of names section
    C. classified directory   D. information services

16.____

17. According to the information in the above passage for locating government agencies, the   17._____
    Information Office of the Department of Consumer Affairs of New York City government
    would be alphabetically listed FIRST under

    A.   *I* for Information Offices
    B.   *D* for Department of Consumer Affairs
    C.   *N* for New York City
    D.   *G* for government

18. When the name of a business is known, the QUICKEST way to find the phone number is   18.__ _
    to look in the

    A.   classified directory
    B.   introductory section
    C.   alphabetical listing of names section
    D.   advertising service section

19. The QUICKEST way to find the phone number of a business when the type of service a   19._____
    business offers and its address is known is to look in the

    A.   classified directory
    B.   alphabetical listing of names section
    C.   introductory section
    D.   information service

20. What is a *telltale?*   20._____

    A.   An alphabetical listing
    B.   A guide name
    C.   A map
    D.   A cross-reference listing

21. The BEST way to find a postal zip code is to look in the   21._____

    A.   classified directory
    B.   introductory section
    C.   alphabetical listing of names section
    D.   government heading

22. To help find names which have several different spellings, the telephone directory pro-   22._____
    vides

    A.   cross-reference spelling   B.   *telltales*
    C.   spelling guides   D.   advertising services

23. Assume that your agency has been given $2025 to purchase file cabinets.   23._____
    If each file cabinet costs $135, how many file cabinets can your agency purchase?

    A.   8   B.   10   C.   15   D.   16

24. Assume that your unit ordered 14 staplers at a total cost of $30.20, and each stapler cost   24.____
the same.
The cost of one stapler was MOST NEARLY

    A. $1.02   B. $1.61   C. $2.16   D. $2.26

25. Assume that you are responsible for counting and recording licensing fees collected by   25.____
your department. On a particular day, your department collected in fees 40 checks in the
amount of $6 each, 80 checks in the amount of $4 each, 45 twenty dollar bills, 30 ten dollar bills, 42 five dollar bills, and 186 one dollar bills.
The TOTAL amount in fees collected on that day was

    A. $1,406   B. $1,706   C. $2,156   D. $2,356

26. Assume that you are responsible for your agency's petty cash fund. During the month of   26.____
February, you pay out 7 $2.00 subway fares and one taxi fare for $10.85. You pay out
nothing else from the fund. At the end of February, you count the money left in the fund
and find 3 one dollar bills, 4 quarters, 5 dimes, and 4 nickels. The amount of money you
had available in the petty cash fund at the BEGINNING of February was

    A. $4.70   B. $16.35   C. $24.85   D. $29.55

27. You overhear your supervisor criticize a co-worker for handling equipment in an unsafe   27.____
way. You feel that the criticism may be unfair.
Of the following, it would be BEST for you to

    A. take your co-worker aside and tell her how you feel about your supervisor's com-
        ments
    B. interrupt the discussion and defend your co-worker to your supervisor
    C. continue working as if you had not overheard the discussion
    D. make a list of other workers who have violated safety rules and give it to your
        supervisor

28. Assume that you have been assigned to work on a long-term project with an employee   28.____
who is known for being uncooperative.
In beginning to work with this employee, it would be LEAST desirable for you to

    A. understand why the person is uncooperative
    B. act in a calm manner rather than an emotional manner
    C. be appreciative of the co-worker's work
    D. report the co-worker's lack of cooperation to your supervisor

29. Assume that you are assigned to sell tickets at a city-owned ice skating rink. An adult   29.____
ticket costs $4.50, and a children's ticket costs $2.25. At the end of a day, you find that
you have sold 36 adult tickets and 80 children's tickets.
The TOTAL amount of money you collected for that day was

    A. $244.80   B. $318.00   C. $342.00   D. $348.00

30. If each office worker files 487 index cards in one hour, how many cards can 26 office   30.____
workers file in one hour?

    A. 10,662   B. 12,175   C. 12,662   D. 14,200

KEY (CORRECT ANSWERS)

1.	D		16.	C
2.	B		17.	C
3.	A		18.	C
4.	D		19.	A
5.	A		20.	B
6.	A		21.	B
7.	C		22.	A
8.	B		23.	C
9.	A		24.	C
10.	C		25.	C
11.	C		26.	D
12.	D		27.	C
13.	A		28.	D
14.	C		29.	C
15.	D		30.	C

———

EXAMINATION SECTION
TEST 1

DIRECTIONS: Each question or incomplete statement is followed by several suggested answers or completions. Select the one that BEST answers the question or completes the statement. *PRINT THE LETTER OF THE CORRECT ANSWER IN THE SPACE AT THE RIGHT.*

Questions 1-2.

DIRECTIONS: Questions 1 and 2 are to be answered on the basis of the following conditions.

Assume that you work for Department A, which occupies several floors in one building. There is a reception office on each floor. All visitors (persons not employed in the department) are required to go to the reception office on the same floor as the office of the person they want to see. They sign a register, their presence is announced by the receptionist, and they wait in the reception room for the person they are visiting.

1. As you are walking in the corridor of your department on your way to a meeting in Room 314, a visitor approaches you and asks you to direct her to Room 312. She says that she is delivering some papers to Mr. Crane in that office. The MOST APPROPRIATE action for you to take is to

   A. offer to deliver the papers to Mr. Crane since you will be passing his office
   B. suggest that she come with you since you will be passing Room 312
   C. direct her to the reception office where Mr. Crane will be contacted for her
   D. take her to the reception office and contact Mr. Crane for her

   1.____

2. You are acting as receptionist in the reception office on the second floor. A man enters, stating that he is an accountant from another department and that he has an appointment with Mr. Prince, who is located in Room 102 on the first floor.
   The BEST action for you to take is to

   A. phone the reception office on the first floor and ask the receptionist to contact Mr. Prince
   B. advise the man to go to the reception office on the first floor where he will be further assisted
   C. contact Mr. Prince for him and ask that he come to your office where his visitor is waiting
   D. send him directly to Room 102 where he can see Mr. Prince

   2.____

3. One of the employees whom you supervise complains to you that you give her more work than the other employees and that she cannot finish these assignments by the time you expect them to be completed.
   Of the following, the FIRST action you should then take is to

   A. tell the employee that you expect more work from her because the other employees do not have her capabilities
   B. assure the employee that you always divide the work equally among your subordinates

   3.____

    C.   review the employee's recent assignments in order to determine whether her complaint is justified

    D.   ask the employee if there are any personal problems which are interfering with the completion of the assignments

4.   Assume that a staff regulation exists which requires an employee to inform his supervisor if the employee will be absent on a particular day.
If an employee fails to follow this regulation, the FIRST action his supervisor should take is to

    A.   inform his own supervisor of the situation and ask for further instructions

    B.   ask the employee to explain his failure to follow the regulation

    C.   tell the employee that another breach of the regulation will lead to disciplinary action

    D.   reprimand the employee for failing to follow the regulation

4.____

5.   An employee tells his supervisor that he submitted an idea to the employees' suggestion program by mail over two months ago and still has not received an indication that the suggestion is being considered. The employee states that when one of his co-workers sent in a suggestion, he received a response within one week. The employee then asks his supervisor what he should do.
Which of the following is the BEST response for the supervisor to make?

    A.   "Next time you have a suggestion, see me about it first and I will make sure that it is properly handled."

    B.   "I'll try to find out whether your suggestion was received by the program and whether a response was sent."

    C.   "Your suggestion probably wasn't that good so there's no sense in pursuing the matter any further."

    D.   "Let's get together and submit the suggestion jointly so that it will carry more weight."

5.____

6.   Assume that you have been trying to teach a newly appointed employee the filing procedures used in your office. The employee seems to be having difficulty learning the procedures even though you consider them relatively simple and you originally learned them in less time than you have already spent trying to teach the new employee.
Before you spend any time trying to teach him any new filing procedures, which of the following actions should you take FIRST?

    A.   Try to teach him some other aspect of your office's work.

    B.   Tell him that you had little difficulty learning the procedures and ask him why he finds them so hard to learn.

    C.   Review with him those procedures you have tried to teach him and determine whether he understands them.

    D.   Report to your supervisor that the new employee is unsuited for the work performed in your office.

6.____

7.   There is a rule in your office that all employees must sign in and out for lunch. You notice that a new employee who is under your direct supervision has not signed in or out for lunch for the past three days. Of the following, the MOST effective action to take is to

7.____

A. immediately report this matter to your supervisor
B. note this infraction of rules on the employee's personnel record
C. remind the employee that she must sign in and out for lunch every day
D. send around a memorandum to all employees in the office telling them they must sign in and out for lunch every day

Questions 8-15.

DIRECTIONS: Questions 8 through 15 each show in Column I names written on four cards (lettered w, x, y, z) which have to be filed. You are to choose the option (lettered A, B, C, or D) in Column II which BEST represents the proper order of filing according to the rules and sample question given below. The cards are to be filed according to the following Rules for Alphabetical Filing.

RULES FOR ALPHABETICAL FILING

Names of Individuals

1. The names of individuals are filed in strict alphabetical order, first according to the last name, then according to first name or initial, and finally according to middle name or initial. For example: George Allen precedes Edward Bell and Leonard Reston precedes Lucille Reston.

2. When last names are the same, for example, A. Green and Agnes Green, the one with the initial comes before the one with the name written out when the first initials are identical.

3. When first and last names are the same, a name without a middle initial comes before one with a middle initial. For example: Ralph Simon comes before both Ralph A. Simon and Ralph Adam Simon.

4. When first and last names are the same, a name with a middle initial comes before one with a middle name beginning with the same initial. For example: Sam P. Rogers comes before Sam Paul Rogers.

5. Prefixes such as De , O', Mac, Mc, and Van are filed as written and are treated as part of the names to which they are connected. For example: Gladys McTeaque is filed before Frances Meadows.

6. Abbreviated names are treated as if they were spelled out. For example: Chas. is filed as Charles and Thos. is filed as Thomas.

7. Titles and designations such as Dr., Mr., and Prof, are ignored in filing.

Names of Organizations

1. The names of business organizations are filed according to the order in which each word in the name appears. When an organization name bears the name of a person, it is filed according to the rules for filing names of people as given above. Vivian Quinn Boutique would, therefore, come before Security Locks Inc. because Quinn comes before Security.

2. When numerals occur in a name, they are treated as if they were spelled out. For example: 4th Street Thrift Shop is filed as Fourth Street Thrift Shop.

3. When the following words are part of the name of an organization, they are ignored: on, the, of, and.

SAMPLE

	Column I	Column II	The correct way to file the cards is:
w.	Jane Earl	A. w, y, z, x	y. James Earl
x.	James A. Earle	B. y, w, z, x	w. Jane Earl
y.	James Earl	C. x, y, w, z	z. J. Earle
z.	J. Earle	D. x, w, y, z	x. James A. Earle

The correct filing order is shown by the letters, y, w, z, x (in that sequence). Since, in Column II, B appears in front of the letters, y, w, z, x (in that sequence), B is the correct answer to the sample question.

Now answer the following questions using that same procedure.

Column I   Column II

8. w. James Rothschild   A. x, z, w, y   8._____
    x. Julius B. Rothchild   B. x, w, z, y
    y. B. Rothstein   C. z, y, w, x
    z. Brian Joel Rothenstein   D. z, w, x, y

9. w. George S. Wise   A. w, y, z, x   9._____
    x. S. G. Wise   B. x , w , y , z
    y. Geo. Stuart Wise   C. y, x, w, z
    z. Prof. Diana Wise   D. z, w, y, x

10. w. 10th Street Bus Terminal   A. x, z, w, y   10._____
    x. Buckingham Travel Agency   B. y, x, w, z
    y. The Buckingham Theater   C. w, z, y, x
    z. Burt Tompkins Studio   D. x, w, y, z

11. w. National Council of American A. w, y, x, z   11._____
       Importers   B. x, z, w, y
    x. National Chain Co. of Provi- C. z, x, w, y
       dence   D. z, x, y, w
    y. National Council on Alcoholism
    z. National Chain Co.

12. w. Dr. Herbert Alvary   A. w, y, x, z   12._____
    x. Mr. Victor Alvarado   B. z, w, x, y
    y. Alvar Industries   C. y, z, x, w
    z. V. Alvarado   D. w, z, x, y

Column I	Column II	
13. w. Joan MacBride	A. w, x, z, y	13._____
x. Wm. Mackey	B. w, y, z, x	
y. Roslyn McKenzie	C. w, z, x, y	
z. Winifred Mackey	D. w, y , x, z	

Column I	Column II	
14. w. 3 Way Trucking Co.	A. y, x, z, w	14._____
x. 3rd Street Bakery	B. y, z, w, x	
y. 380 Realty Corp.	C. x, y, z, w	
z. Three Lions Pub	D. x, y, w, z	

15. w. Miss Rose Leonard	A. z, w, x, y	15._____
x. Rev. Leonard Lucas	B. w, z, y, x	
y. Sylvia Leonard Linen Shop	C. w, x, z, y	
z. Rose S. Leonard	D. z, w, y, x	

Questions 16-19.

DIRECTIONS: Answer Questions 16 through 19 ONLY on the basis of the information given in the following passage.

Work measurement concerns accomplishment or productivity. It has to do with results; it does not deal with the amount of energy used up, although in many cases this may be in direct proportion to the work output. Work measurement not only helps a manager to distribute work loads fairly, but it also enables him to define work sueeess in actual units, evaluate employee performance, and determine where corrective help is needed. Work measurement is accomplished by measuring the amount produced, measuring the time spent to produce it, and relating the two. To illustrate, it is common to speak of so many orders processed within a given time. The number of orders processed becomes meaningful when related to the amount of time taken.

Much of the work in an office can be measured fairly accurately and inexpensively. The extent of wo.rk measurement possible in any given case will depend upon the particular type of office tasks performed, but usually from two-thirds to three-fourths of all work in an office can be measured. It is true that difficulty in work measurement is encountered, for example, when the office work is irregular and not repeated often, or when the work is primarily mental rather than manual. These are problems, but they are used as excuses for doing no work measurement far more frequently than is justified.

16. According to the above passage, which of the following BEST illustrates the type of information obtained as a result of work measurement? A   16._____

    A. clerk takes one hour to file 150 folders
    B. typist types five letters
    C. stenographer works harder typing from shorthand notes than she does typing from a typed draft
    D. clerk keeps track of employees' time by computing sick leave, annual leave, and overtime leave

17. The above passage does NOT indicate that work measurement can be used to help a   17.____
    supervisor to determine

    A. why an employee is performing poorly on the job
    B. who are the fast and slow workers in the unit
    C. how the work in the unit should be divided up
    D. how long it should take to perform a certain task

18. According to the above passage, the kind of work that would be MOST difficult to mea-   18.____
    sure would be such work as

    A. sorting mail
    B. designing a form for a new procedure
    C. photocopying various materials
    D. answering inquiries with form letters

19. The excuses mentioned in the above passage for failure to perform work measurement   19.____
    can be BEST summarized as the

    A. repetitive nature of office work
    B. costs involved in carrying out accurate work measurement
    C. inability to properly use the results obtained from work measurement
    D. difficulty involved in measuring certain types of work

Questions 20-24.

DIRECTIONS: In each of Questions 20 through 24, there is a sentence containing one under-
              lined word. Choose the word (lettered A, B, C, or D) which means MOST
              NEARLY the same as the underlined word as it is used in the sentence.

20. Mr. Warren could not attend the luncheon because he had a prior appointment.   20.____

    A. conflicting   B. official
    C. previous   D. important

21. The time allowed to complete the task was not adequate.   21.____

    A. long   B. enough   C. excessive   D. required

22. The investigation unit began an extensive search for the information.   22.____

    A. complicated   B. superficial
    C. thorough   D. leisurely

23. The secretary answered the telephone in a courteous manner.   23.____

    A. businesslike   B. friendly
    C. formal   D. polite

24. The recipient of the money checked the total amount.   24.____

    A. receiver   B. carrier   C. borrower   D. giver

25. You receive a telephone call from an employee in another agency requesting information 25.____
about a project being carried out by a division other than your own. You know little about
the work being done, but you would like to help the caller.
Of the following, the BEST action for you to take is to

   A. ask the caller exactly what he would like to know and then tell him all you know
   about the work being done
   B. ask the caller to tell you exactly what he would like to know so that you can get the
   information while he waits
   C. tell the caller that you will have the call transferred to the division working on the
   project
   D. request that the caller write to you so that you can send him the necessary information

---

KEY (CORRECT ANSWERS)

1.	C		11.	D
2.	B		12.	C
3.	C		13.	A
4.	B		14.	C
5.	B		15.	B
6.	C		16.	A
7.	C		17.	A
8.	A		18.	B
9.	D		19.	D
10.	B		20.	C

21.	B
22.	C
23.	D
24.	A
25.	C

TEST 2

DIRECTIONS: Each question or incomplete statement is followed by several suggested answers or completions. Select the one that BEST answers the question or completes the statement. *PRINT THE LETTER OF THE CORRECT ANSWER IN THE SPACE AT THE RIGHT.*

1. Which of the following actions by a supervisor is LEAST likely to result in an increase in morale or productivity?   1._____

   A. Delegating additional responsibility but not authority to his subordinates
   B. Spending more time than his subordinates in planning and organizing the office's work
   C. Giving positive rather than negative orders to his subordinates
   D. Keeping his subordinates informed about changes in rules or policies which affect their work

Questions 2-8.

DIRECTIONS: Questions 2 through 8 are based SOLELY on the information and the form given below.

The following form is a *Weekly Summary of New Employees* and lists all employees appointed to Department F in the week indicated. In addition to the starting date and name, the form includes each new employee's time card number, title, status, work location and supervisor's name.

DEPARTMENT F						
Weekly Summary of New Employees					Week Starting March 25	
Start-ing Date	Name Last, First	Time Card No.	Title	Status	Work Location	Supervisor
3/25	Astaire, Hannah	361	Typist	Prov.	Rm. 312	Merrill, Judy
3/25	Silber, Arthur	545	Clerk	Perm.	Rm. 532	Rizzo, Joe
3/26	Vecchio, Robert	620	Accountant	Perm.	Rm. 620	Harper, Ruth
3/26	Goldberg, Sally	373	Stenographer	Prov.	Rm. 308	Merrill, Judy
3/26	Yee, Bruce	555	Accountant	Perm.	Rm. 530	Rizzo, Joe
3/27	Dunning, Betty	469	Typist	Perm.	Rm. 411	Miller, Tony
3/28	Goldman, Sara	576	Stenographer	Prov.	Rm. 532	Rizzo, Joe
3/29	Vesquez, Roy	624	Accountant	Perm.	Rm. 622	Harper, Ruth
3/29	Browning, David	464	Typist	Perm.	Rm. 411	Miller, Tony

2. On which one of the following dates did two employees *in the same title* begin work?　　2.____

    A.　3/25　　　　B.　3/26　　　　C.　3/27　　　　D.　3/29

3. To which one of the following supervisors was ONE typist assigned?　　3.____

    A.　Judy Merrill　　　　　　　B.　Tony Miller
    C.　Ruth Harper　　　　　　　D.　Joe Rizzo

4. Which one of the following supervisors was assigned the GREATEST number of new　　4.____
employees during the week of March 25?

    A.　Ruth Harper　　　　　　　B.　Judy Merrill
    C.　Tony Miller　　　　　　　D.　Joe Rizzo

5. Which one of the following employees was assigned *three days after another employee*　　5.____
·to the same job location?

    A.　Sara Goldman　　　　　　B.　David Browning
    C.　Bruce Yee　　　　　　　　D.　Roy Vesquez

6. The title in which BOTH provisional and permanent appointments were made is　　6.____

    A.　accountant　　B.　clerk　　　　C.　stenographer　　D.　typist

7. The employee who started work on the SAME day and have the SAME status but DIF-　　7.____
FERENT titles are

    A.　Arthur Silber and Hannah Astaire
    B.　Robert Vecchio and Bruce Yee
    C.　Sally Goldberg and Sara Goldman
    D.　Roy Vesquez and David Browning

8. On the basis of the information given on the form, which one of the following conclusions　　8.____
regarding time card numbers appears to be CORRECT?

    A.　The first digit of the time card number is coded according to the assigned title.
    B.　The middle digit of the time card number is coded according to the assigned title.
    C.　The first digit of the time card number is coded according to the employees' floor
       locations.
    D.　Time card numbers are randomly assigned.

9. Assume that a caller arrives at your desk and states that she is your supervisor's daugh-　　9.____
ter and that she would like to see her father. You have been under the impression that
your supervisor has only a two-year-old son.
Of the following, the BEST way to deal with this visitor is to

    A.　offer her a seat and advise your supervisor of the visitor
    B.　tell her to go right in to her father's office
    C.　ask her for some proof to show that she is your supervisor's daughter
    D.　escort her into your supervisor's office and ask him if the visitor is his daughter

10. Assume that you answer the telephone and the caller says that he is a police officer and　　10.____
asks for personal information about one of your co-workers.
Of the following, the BEST course of action for you to take is to

A. give the caller the information he has requested
B. ask the caller for the telephone number of the phone he is using, call him back, and then give him the information
C. refuse to give him any information and offer to transfer the call to your supervisor
D. ask the caller for his name and badge number before giving him the information

Questions 11-16.

DIRECTIONS: Questions 11 through 16 each consist of a sentence which may or may not be an example of good English usage. Consider grammar, punctuation, spelling, capitalization, awkwardness, etc. Examine each sentence, and then choose the correct statement about it from the four choices below it. If the English usage in the sentence given is better than it would be with any of the changes suggested in Options B, C, or D, choose Option A. Do not choose an option that will change the meaning of the sentence.

11. The recruiting officer said, *"There are many different goverment jobs available."*   11.____

    A. This is an example of acceptable writing.
    B. The word *There* should not be capitalized.
    C. The word *goverment* should be spelled *government*.
    D. The comma after the word *said* should be removed.

12. He can recommend a mechanic whose work is reliable.   12.____

    A. This is an example of acceptable writing.
    B. The word *reliable* should be spelled *relyable*.
    C. The word *whose* should be spelled *who's*.
    D. The word *mechanic* should be spelled *mecanic*.

13. She typed quickly; like someone who had not a moment to lose.   13.____

    A. This is an example of acceptable writing.
    B. The word *not* should be removed.
    C. The semicolon should be changed to a comma.
    D. The word *quickly* should be placed before instead of after the word *typed*.

14. She insisted that she had to much work to do.   14.____

    A. This is an example of acceptable writing.
    B. The word *insisted* should be spelled *incisted*.
    C. The word *to* used in front of *much* should be spelled *too*.
    D. The word *do* should be changed to *be done*.

15. He excepted praise from his supervisor for a job well done.   15.____

    A. This is an example of acceptable writing.
    B. The word *excepted* should be spelled *accepted*.
    C. The order of the words *well done* should be changed to *done well*.
    D. There should be a comma after the word, *supervisor*

16. What appears to be intentional errors in grammar occur several times in the passage.   16._____

    A. This is an example of acceptable writing.
    B. The word *occur* should be spelled *occurr.*
    C. The word *appears* should be changed to *appear.*
    D. The phrase *several times* should be changed to *from time to time.*

17. The daily compensation to be paid to each consultant hired in a certain agency is com-   17._____
puted by dividing his professional earnings in the previous year by 250. The maximum
daily compensation they can receive is $200 each. Four consultants who were hired to
work on a special project had the following professional earnings in the previous year:
$37,500, $44,000, $46,500, and $61,100.
What will be the TOTAL DAILY COST to the agency for these four consultants?

    A. $932   B. $824   C. $756   D. $712

18. In a typing and stenographic pool consisting of 30 employees, 2/5 of them are typists,   18._____
1/3 of them are senior typists and senior stenographers, and the rest are stenographers.
If there are 5 more stenographers than senior stenographers, how many senior stenographers are in the typing and stenographic pool?

    A. 3   B. 5   C. 8   D. 10

19. There are 3330 copies of a three-page report to be collated. One clerk starts collating at   19._____
9:00 A.M. and is joined 15 minutes later by two other clerks. It takes 15 minutes for each
of these clerks to collate 90 copies of the report.
At what time should the job be completed if ALL three clerks continue working at the
SAME rate without breaks?

    A. 12:00 Noon   B. 12:15 P.M.   C. 1:00 P.M.   D. 1:15 P.M.

20. By the end of last year, membership in the blood credit program in a certain agency had   20._____
increased from the year before by 500, bringing the total to 2500.
If the membership increased by the same percentage this year, the TOTAL number of
members in the blood credit program for this agency by the end of this year should be

    A. 2625   B. 3000   C. 3125   D. 3250

21. During this year, an agency suggestion program put into practice suggestions from 24   21._____
employees, thereby saving the agency 40 times the amount of money it paid in awards.
If 1/3 of the employees were awarded $50 each, 1/2 of the employees were awarded
$25 each, and the rest were awarded $10 each, how much money did the agency
SAVE by using the suggestions?

    A. $18,760   B. $29,600   C. $32,400   D. $46,740

22. Which of the following actions should a supervisor generally find MOST effective as a   22._____
method of determining whether subordinates need additional training in performing their
work?

    A. Compiling a list of absences and latenesses of subordinates
    B. Observing the manner in which his subordinates carry out their various tasks
    C. Reviewing the grievances submitted by subordinates
    D. Reminding his subordinates to consult him if they experience difficulty in complet-
ing an assignment

23. Of the following types of letters, the MOST difficult to trace if lost after mailing is the _____ letter.   23._____

    A. special delivery   B. registered
    C. insured   D. certified

24. Suppose that you are looking over a few incoming letters that have been put in your mail   24._____
basket. You see that one has a return address on the envelope but not on the letter itself.
Of the following, the BEST way to make sure there is a correct record of the return
address is to

    A. return the letter to the sender and ask him to fill in his address on his own letter
    B. put the letter back into the envelope and close the opening with a paper clip
    C. copy the address onto a 3"x5" index card and throw away the envelope
    D. copy the address onto the letter and staple the envelope to the letter

25. Although most incoming mail that you receive in an office will pertain to business mat-   25._____
ters, there are times when a letter may be delivered for your supervisor that is marked
Personal.
Of the following, the BEST way for you to handle this type of mail is to

    A. open the letter but do not read it, and route it along with the other mail
    B. read the letter to see if it really is personal
    C. have the letter forwarded unopened to your supervisor's home address
    D. deliver the letter to your supervisor's desk unopened

KEY (CORRECT ANSWERS)

1.	A		11.	C
2.	B		12.	A
3.	A		13.	C
4.	D		14.	C
5.	A		15.	B
6.	D		16.	C
7.	D		17.	D
8.	C		18.	A
9.	A		19.	B
10.	C		20.	C

21.	B
22.	B
23.	D
24.	D
25.	D

EXAMINATION SECTION
TEST 1

DIRECTIONS: Each question or incomplete statement is followed by several suggested answers or completions. Select the one that BEST answers the question or completes the statement. *PRINT THE LETTER OF THE CORRECT ANSWER IN THE SPACE AT THE RIGHT.*

1. A push-button telephone with six buttons, one of which is a *hold* button, is often used when more than one outside line is needed.
    If you are talking on one line of this type of telephone when another call comes in, what is the procedure to follow if you want to answer the second call but keep the first call on the line? Push the   1._____

    A. *hold* button at the same time as you push the *pickup* button of the ringing line
    B. *hold* button and then push the *pickup* button of the ringing line
    C. *pickup* button of the ringing line and then push the *hold* button
    D. *pickup* button of the ringing line and push the *hold* button when you return to the original line

2. Suppose that you are asked to prepare a petty cash statement for March. The original and one copy are to go to the personnel office. One copy is to go to the fiscal office, and another copy is to go to your supervisor. The last copy is for your files.
    In preparing the statement and the copies, how many sheets of copy paper should you use?   2._____

    A. 3   B. 4   C. 5   D. 8

3. Which one of the following is the LEAST important advantage of putting the subject of a letter in the heading to the right of the address?
    It   3._____

    A. makes filing of the copy easier
    B. makes more space available in the body of the letter
    C. simplifies distribution of letters
    D. simplifies determination of the subject of the letter

4. Of the following, the MOST efficient way to put 100 copies of a one-page letter into 9 1/2" x 4 1/8" envelopes for mailing is to fold _____ into an envelope.   4._____

    A. each letter and insert it immediately after folding
    B. each letter separately until all 100 are folded; then insert each one
    C. the 100 letters two at a time, then separate them and insert each one
    D. two letters together, slip them apart, and insert each one

5. When preparing papers for filing, it is NOT desirable to   5._____

    A. smooth papers that are wrinkled
    B. use paper clips to keep related papers together in the files
    C. arrange the papers in the order in which they will be filed
    D. mend torn papers with cellophane tape

6. Of the following, the BEST reason for a clerical unit to have its own duplicating machine is that the unit

    6.____

    A. uses many forms which it must reproduce internally
    B. must make two copies of each piece of incoming mail for a special file
    C. must make seven copies of each piece of outgoing mail
    D. must type 200 envelopes each month for distribution to the same offices

7. Several offices use the same photocopying machine.
If each office must pay its share of the cost of running this machine, the BEST way of determining how much of this cost should be charged to each of these offices is to

    7.____

    A. determine the monthly number of photocopies made by each office
    B. determine the monthly number of originals submitted for photocopying by each office
    C. determine the number of times per day each office uses the photocopy machine
    D. divide the total cost of running the photocopy machine by the total number of offices using the machine

8. Which one of the following would it be BEST to use to indicate that a file folder has been removed from the files for temporary use in another office?
A(n)

    8.____

    A. cross-reference card   B. tickler file marker
    C. aperture card   D. out guide

9. Which one of the following is the MOST important objective of filing?

    9.____

    A. Giving a secretary something to do in her spare time
    B. Making it possible to locate information quickly
    C. Providing a place to store unneeded documents
    D. Keeping extra papers from accumulating on workers' desks

10. If a check has been made out for an incorrect amount, the BEST action for the writer of the check to take is to

    10.____

    A. erase the original amount and enter the correct amount
    B. cross out the original amount with a single line and enter the correct amount above it
    C. black out the original amount so that it cannot be read and enter the correct amount above it
    D. write a new check

11. Which one of the following BEST describes the usual arrangement of a tickler file?

    11.____

    A. Alphabetical   B. Chronological
    C. Numerical   D. Geographical

12. Which one of the following is the LEAST desirable filing practice?

    12.____

    A. Using staples to keep papers together
    B. Filing all material without regard to date
    C. Keeping a record of all materials removed from the files
    D. Writing filing instructions on each paper prior to filing

13. Assume that one of your duties is to keep records of the office supplies used by your unit   13.____
for the purpose of ordering new supplies when the old supplies run out. The information
that will be of MOST help in letting you know when to reorder supplies is the

    A. quantity issued   B. quantity received
    C. quantity on hand   D. stock number

Questions 14-19.

DIRECTIONS: Questions 14 through 19 consist of sets of names and addresses. In each
question, the name and address in Column II should be an exact copy of the
name and address in Column I. If there is:
a mistake *only* in the name, mark your answer A;
a mistake *only* in the address, mark your answer B;
a mistake in *both* name and address, mark your answer C;
no mistake in *either* name or address, mark your answer D.

SAMPLE QUESTION

Column I
Michael Filbert
456 Reade Street
New York, N.Y. 10013

Column II
Michael Filbert
645 Reade Street
New York, N.Y. 10013

Since there is a mistake only in the address (the street number should be 456
instead of 645), the answer to the sample question is B.

COLUMN I   COLUMN II

14. Esta Wong   Esta Wang   14.____
141 West 68 St.   141 West 68 St.
New York, N.Y. 10023   New York, N.Y. 10023

15. Dr. Alberto Grosso   Dr. Alberto Grosso   15.____
3475 12th Avenue   3475 12th Avenue
Brooklyn, N.Y. 11218   Brooklyn, N.Y. 11218

16. Mrs. Ruth Bortlas   Ms. Ruth Bortlas   16.____
482 Theresa Ct.   482 Theresa Ct.
Far Rockaway, N.Y. 11691   Far Rockaway, N.Y. 11169

17. Mr. and Mrs. Howard Fox   Mr. and Mrs. Howard Fox   17.____
2301 Sedgwick Ave.   231 Sedgwick Ave.
Bronx, N.Y. 10468   Bronx, N.Y. 10468

18. Miss Marjorie Black   Miss Margorie Black   18.____
223 East 23 Street   223 East 23 Street
New York, N.Y. 10010   New York, N.Y. 10010

19. Michelle Herman   Michelle Hermann   19.____
806 Valley Rd.   806 Valley Dr.
Old Tappan, N.J. 07675   Old Tappan, N.J. 07675

Questions 20-25.

DIRECTIONS: Questions 20 through 25 are to be answered SOLELY on the basis of the information in the following passage.

Basic to every office is the need for proper lighting. Inadequate lighting is a familiar cause of fatigue and serves to create a somewhat dismal atmosphere in the office. One requirement of proper lighting is that it be of an appropriate intensity. Intensity is measured in foot-candles. According to the Illuminating Engineering Society of New York, for casual seeing tasks such as in reception rooms, inactive file rooms, and other service areas, it is recommended that the amount of light be 30 foot-candles. For ordinary seeing tasks such as reading and work in active file rooms and in mail rooms, the recommended lighting is 100 foot-candles. For very difficult seeing tasks such as accounting, transcribing, and business machine use, the recommended lighting is 150 foot-candles.

Lighting intensity is only one requirement. Shadows and glare are to be avoided. For example, the larger the proportion of a ceiling filled with lighting units, the more glare-free and comfortable the lighting will be. Natural lighting from windows is not too dependable because on dark wintry days, windows yield little usable light, and on sunny, summer afternoons, the glare from windows may be very distracting. Desks should not face the windows. Finally, the main lighting source ought to be overhead and to the left of the user.

20.   According to the above passage, insufficient light in the office may cause   20.____

       A. glare   B. shadows
       C. tiredness   D. distraction

21.   Based on the above passage, which of the following must be considered when planning   21.____
       lighting arrangements?
       The

       A. amount of natural light present
       B. amount of work to be done
       C. level of difficulty of work to be done
       D. type of activity to be carried out

22.   It can be inferred from the above passage that a well-coordinated lighting scheme is   22.____
       LIKELY to result in

       A. greater employee productivity
       B. elimination of light reflection
       C. lower lighting cost
       D. more use of natural light

23.   Of the following, the BEST title for the above passage is   23.____

       A. Characteristics of Light
       B. Light Measurement Devices
       C. Factors to Consider When Planning Lighting Systems
       D. Comfort vs. Cost When Devising Lighting Arrangements

24. According to the above passage, a foot-candle is a measurement of the

    A. number of bulbs used
    B. strength of the light
    C. contrast between glare and shadow
    D. proportion of the ceiling filled with lighting units

24.____

25. According to the above passage, the number of foot-candles of light that would be needed to copy figures onto a payroll is _____ foot-candles.

    A. less than 30   B. 30
    C. 100   D. 150

25.____

KEY (CORRECT ANSWERS)

1.	B	11.	B
2.	B	12.	B
3.	B	13.	C
4.	A	14.	A
5.	B	15.	D
6.	A	16.	C
7.	A	17.	B
8.	D	18.	A
9.	B	19.	C
10.	D	20.	C

21.	D
22.	A
23.	C
24.	B
25.	D

TEST 2

DIRECTIONS: Each question or incomplete statement is followed by several suggested answers or completions. Select the one that BEST answers the question or completes the statement. *PRINT THE LETTER OF THE CORRECT ANSWER IN THE SPACE AT THE RIGHT.*

1. Assume that a supervisor has three subordinates who perform clerical tasks. One of the employees retires and is replaced by someone who is transferred from another unit in the agency. The transferred employee tells the supervisor that she has worked as a clerical employee for two years and understands clerical operations quite well. The supervisor then assigns the transferred employee to a desk, tells the employee to begin working, and returns to his own desk.
The supervisor's action in this situation is

   A. *proper;* experienced clerical employees do not require training when they are transferred to new assignments
   B. *improper;* before the supervisor returns to his desk, he should tell the other two subordinates to watch the transferred employee perform the work
   C. *proper;* if the transferred employee makes any mistakes, she will bring them to the supervisor's attention
   D. *improper;* the supervisor should find out what clerical tasks the transferred employee has performed and give her instruction in those which are new or different

2. Assume that you are falling behind in completing your work assignments and you believe that your workload is too heavy.
Of the following, the BEST course of action for you to take FIRST is to

   A. discuss the problem with your supervisor
   B. decide which of your assignments can be postponed
   C. try to get some of your co-workers to help you out
   D. plan to take some of the work home with you in order to catch up

3. Suppose that one of the clerks under your supervision is filling in monthly personnel forms. She asks you to explain a particular personnel regulation which is related to various items on the forms. You are not thoroughly familiar with the regulation.
Of the following responses you may make, the one which will gain the MOST respect from the clerk and which is generally the MOST advisable is to

   A. tell the clerk to do the best she can and that you will check her work later
   B. inform the clerk that you are not sure of a correct explanation but suggest a procedure for her to follow
   C. give the clerk a suitable interpretation so that she will think you are familiar with all regulations
   D. tell the clerk that you will have to read the regulation more thoroughly before you can give her an explanation

4. Charging out records until a specified due date, with prompt follow-up if they are not returned, is a

A. *good* idea; it may prevent the records from being kept needlessly on someone's desk for long periods of time
B. *good* idea; it will indicate the extent of your authority to other departments
C. *poor* idea; the person borrowing the material may make an error because of the pressure put upon him to return the records
D. *poor* idea; other departments will feel that you do not trust them with the records and they will be resentful

Questions 5-9.

DIRECTIONS: Questions 5 through 9 consist of three lines of code letters and numbers. The numbers on each line should correspond with the code letters on the same line in accordance with the table below.

Code Letter	P	L	I	J	B	O	H	U	C	G
Corresponding Number	0	1	2	3	4	5	6	7	8	9

On some of the lines, an error exists in the coding. Compare the letters and numbers in each question carefully. If you find an error or errors on
    only *one* of the lines in the question, mark your answer A;
    any *two* lines in the question, mark your answer B;
    all *three* lines in the question, mark your answer C;
    none of the lines in the question, mark your answer D.

SAMPLE QUESTION

JHOILCP   3652180
BICLGUP   4286970
UCIBHLJ   5824613

In the above sample, the first line is correct since each code letter listed has the correct corresponding number. On the second line, an error exists because code letter L should have the number 1 instead of the number 6. On the third line, an error exists because the code letter U should have the number 7 instead of the number 5. Since there are errors on two of the three lines, the correct answer is B.

5. BULJCIP   4713920   5.____
    HIGPOUL   6290571
    OCUHJBI   5876342

6. CUBLOIJ   8741023   6.____
    LCLGCLB   1818914
    JPUHIOC   3076158

7. OIJGCBPO   52398405   7.____
    UHPBLIOP   76041250
    CLUIPGPC   81720908

8. BPCOUOJI   40875732   8._____
    UOHCIPLB   75682014
    GLHUUCBJ   92677843

9. HOIOHJLH   65256361   9._____
    IOJJHHBP   25536640
    OJHBJOPI   53642502

Questions 10-13.

DIRECTIONS: Questions 10 through 13 are to be answered SOLELY on the basis of the information given in the following passage.

The mental attitude of the employee toward safety is exceedingly important in preventing accidents. All efforts designed to keep safety on the employee's mind and to keep accident prevention a live subject in the office will help substantially in a safety program. Although it may seem strange, it is common for people to be careless. Therefore, safety education is a continuous process.

Safety rules should be explained, and the reasons for their rigid enforcement should be given to employees. Telling employees to be careful or giving similar general safety warnings and slogans is probably of little value. Employees should be informed of basic safety fundamentals. This can be done through staff meetings, informal suggestions to employees, movies, and safety instruction cards. Safety instruction cards provide the employees with specific suggestions about safety and serve as a series of timely reminders helping to keep safety on the minds of employees. Pictures, posters, and cartoon sketches on bulletin boards that are located in areas continually used by employees arouse the employees' interest in safety. It is usually good to supplement this type of safety promotion with intensive individual follow-up.

10. The above passage implies that the LEAST effective of the following safety measures is   10._____

     A.   rigid enforcement of safety rules
     B.   getting employees to think in terms of safety
     C.   elimination of unsafe conditions in the office
     D.   telling employees to stay alert at all times

11. The reason given by the passage for maintaining ongoing safety education is that   11._____

     A.   people are often careless
     B.   office tasks are often dangerous
     C.   the value of safety slogans increases with repetition
     D.   safety rules change frequently

12. Which one of the following safety aids is MOST likely to be preferred by the passage?   12._____
     A

     A.   cartoon of a man tripping over a carton and yelling, *Keep aisles clear!*
     B.   poster with a large number one and a caption saying, *Safety First*
     C.   photograph of a very neatly arranged office
     D.   large sign with the word *THINK* in capital letters

13. Of the following, the BEST title for the above passage is   13.____

    A. Basic Safety Fundamentals
    B. Enforcing Safety Among Careless Employees
    C. Attitudes Toward Safety
    D. Making Employees Aware of Safety

Questions 14-21.

DIRECTIONS: Questions 14 through 21 are to be answered SOLELY on the basis of the information and the chart given below.

    The following chart shows expenses in five selected categories for a one-year period, expressed as percentages of these same expenses during the previous year. The chart compares two different offices. In Office T (represented by ▨▨▨▨), a cost reduction program has been tested for the past year. The other office, Office Q (represented by ▨▨▨), served as a control, in that no special effort was made' to reduce costs during the past year.

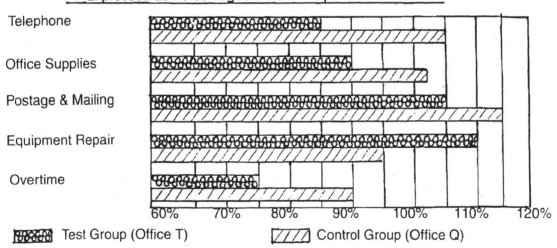

RESULTS OF OFFICE COST REDUCTION PROGRAM

Expenses of Test and Control Groups for 2016
Expressed as Percentages of Same Expenses for 2015

14. In Office T, which category of expense showed the greatest percentage REDUCTION   14.____
from 2015 to 2016?

    A. Telephone   B. Office Supplies
    C. Postage & Mailing   D. Overtime

15. In which expense category did Office T show the BEST results in percentage terms   15.____
when compared to Office Q?

    A. Telephone   B. Office Supplies
    C. Postage & Mailing   D. Overtime

16. According to the above chart, the cost reduction program was LEAST effective for the 16.____
    expense category of

    A. Office Supplies   B. Postage & Mailing
    C. Equipment Repair   D. Overtime

17. Office T's telephone costs went down during 2016 by approximately how many percent- 17.____
    age points?

    A. 15   B. 20   C. 85   D. 105

18. Which of the following changes occurred in expenses for Office Supplies in Office Q in 18.____
    the year 2016 as compared with the year 2015?
    They

    A. increased by more than 100%
    B. remained the same
    C. decreased by a few percentage points
    D. increased by a few percentage points

19. For which of the following expense categories do the results in Office T and the results in 19.____
    Office Q differ MOST NEARLY by 10 percentage points?

    A. Telephone   B. Postage & Mailing
    C. Equipment Repair   D. Overtime

20. In which expense category did Office Q's costs show the GREATEST percentage 20.____
    increase in 2016?

    A. Telephone   B. Office Supplies
    C. Postage & Mailing   D. Equipment Repair

21. In Office T, by approximately what percentage did overtime expense change during the 21.____
    past year?
    It

    A. *increased* by 15%   B. *increased* by 75%
    C. *decreased* by 10%   D. *decreased* by 25%

22. In a particular agency, there were 160 accidents in 2007. Of these accidents, 75% were 22.____
    due to unsafe acts and the rest were due to unsafe conditions. In the following year, a
    special safety program was established. The number of accidents in 2009 due to unsafe
    acts was reduced to 35% of what it had been in 2007.
    How many accidents due to unsafe acts were there in 2009?

    A. 20   B. 36   C. 42   D. 56

23. At the end of every month, the petty cash fund of Agency A is reimbursed for payments 23.____
    made from the fund during the month. During the month of February, the amounts paid
    from the fund were entered on receipts as follows: 10 bus fares of 35¢ each and one taxi
    fare of $3.50.
    At the end of the month, the money left in the fund was in the following denominations:
    15 one dollar bills, 4 quarters, 10 dimes, and 20 nickels.
    If the petty cash fund is reduced by 20% for the following month, how much money will
    there be available in the petty cash fund for March?

    A. $11.00   B. $20.00   C. $21.50   D. $25.00

24. The one of the following records which it would be MOST advisable to keep in alphabeti-   24._____
cal order is a

    A. continuous listing of phone messages, including time and caller, for your supervi-
sor
    B. listing of individuals currently employed by your agency in a particular title
    C. record of purchases paid for by the petty cash fund
    D. dated record of employees who have borrowed material from the files in your office

25. Assume that you have been asked to copy by hand a column of numbers with two deci-   25._____
mal places from one record to another. Each number consists of three, four, and five dig-
its.
In order to copy them quickly and accurately, you should copy

    A. each number exactly, making sure that the column of digits farthest to the right is in
a straight line and all other columns are lined up
    B. the column of digits farthest to the right and then copy the next column of digits
moving from right to left
    C. the column of digits farthest to the left and then copy the next column of digits mov-
ing from left to right
    D. the digits to the right of each decimal point and then copy the digits to the left of
each decimal point

KEY (CORRECT ANSWERS)

1.	D		11.	A
2.	A		12.	A
3.	D		13.	D
4.	A		14.	D
5.	A		15.	A
6.	C		16.	C
7.	D		17.	A
8.	B		18.	D
9.	C		19.	B
10.	D		20.	C

21.	D
22.	C
23.	B
24.	B
25.	A

EXAMINATION SECTION
TEST 1

DIRECTIONS: Each question or incomplete statement is followed by several suggested answers or completions. Select the one that BEST answers the question or completes the statement. *PRINT THE LETTER OF THE CORRECT ANSWER IN THE SPACE AT THE RIGHT.*

Questions 1-10.

WORD MEANING

DIRECTIONS: Each question from 1 to 10 contains a word in capitals followed by four suggested meanings of the word. For each question, choose the best meaning. *PRINT THE LETTER OF THE CORRECT ANSWER IN THE SPACE AT THE RIGHT.*

1. ACCURATE   1.____
    A. correct   B. useful   C. afraid   D. careless

2. ALTER   2.____
    A. copy   B. change   C. report   D. agree

3. DOCUMENT   3.____
    A. outline   B. agreement   C. blueprint   D. record

4. INDICATE   4.____
    A. listen   B. show   C. guess   D. try

5. INVENTORY   5.____
    A. custom   B. discovery   C. warning   D. list

6. ISSUE   6.____
    A. annoy   B. use up   C. give out   D. gain

7. NOTIFY   7.____
    A. inform   B. promise   C. approve   D. strengthen

8. ROUTINE   8.____
    A. path   B. mistake   C. habit   D. journey

9. TERMINATE   9.____
    A. rest   B. start   C. deny   D. end

10. TRANSMIT   10.____
    A. put in   B. send   C. stop   D. go across

Questions 11-15.

READING COMPREHENSION

DIRECTIONS: Questions 11 through 15 test how well you understand what you read. It will be necessary for you to read carefully because your answers to these questions should be based ONLY on the information given in the following paragraphs.

The recipient gains an impression of a typewritten letter before he begins to read the message. Pastors which provide for a good first impression include margins and spacing that are visually pleasing, formal parts of the letter which are correctly placed according to the style of the letter, copy which is free of obvious erasures and over-strikes, and transcript that is even and clear. The problem for the typist is that of how to produce that first, positive impression of her work.

There are several general rules which a typist can follow when she wishes to prepare a properly spaced letter on a sheet of letter-head. Ordinarily, the width of a letter should not be less than four inches nor more than six inches. The side margins should also have a desirable relation to the bottom margin and the space between the letterhead and the body of the letter. Usually the most appealing arrangement is when the side margins are even and the bottom margin is slightly wider than the side margins. In some offices, however, standard line length is used for all business letters, and the secretary then varies the spacing between the date line and the inside address according to the length of the letter.

11. The BEST title for the above paragraphs would be: 11._____

    A. Writing Office Letters
    B. Making Good First Impressions
    C. Judging Well-Typed Letters
    D. Good Placing and Spacing for Office Letters

12. According to the above paragraphs, which of the following might be considered the way 12._____
in which people very quickly judge the quality of work which has been typed? By

    A. measuring the margins to see if they are correct
    B. looking at the spacing and cleanliness of the typescript
    C. scanning the body of the letter for meaning
    D. reading the date line and address for errors

13. What, according to the above paragraphs, would be definitely UNDESIRABLE as the 13._____
average line length of a typed letter?

    A. 4"   B. 5"   C. 6"   D. 7"

14. According to the above paragraphs, when the line length is kept standard, the secretary 14._____

    A. does not have to vary the spacing at all since this also is standard
    B. adjusts the spacing between the date line and inside address for different lengths of letters
    C. uses the longest line as a guideline for spacing between the date line and inside address
    D. varies the number of spaces between the lines

15. According to the above paragraphs, side margins are MOST pleasing when they   15.____

    A. are even and somewhat smaller than the bottom margin
    B. are slightly wider than the bottom margin
    C. vary with the length of the letter
    D. are figured independently from the letterhead and the body of the letter

Questions 16-20.

CODING

DIRECTIONS:

Name of Applicant	H A N G S B R U K E
Test Code	c o m p l e x i t y
File Number	0 1 2 3 4 5 6 7 8 9

Assume that each of the above capital letters is the first letter of the name of an Applicant, that the small letter directly beneath each capital letter is the test code for the Applicant, and that the number directly beneath each code letter is the file number for the Applicant.

In each of the following Questions 16 through 20, the test code letters and the file numbers in Columns 2 and 3 should correspond to the capital letters in Column 1. For each question, look at each column carefully and mark your answer as follows:

    If there is an error only in Column 2, mark your
    answer A.
    If there is an error only in Column 3, mark your
    answer B.
    If there is an error in both Columns 2 and 3, mark
    your answer C.
    If both Columns 2 and 3 are correct, mark your
    answer D.

The following sample question is given to help you understand the procedure.

SAMPLE QUESTION

Column 1	Column 2	Column 3
AKEHN	otyci	18902

In Column 2, the final test code letter *i*. should be *m*. Column 3 is correctly coded to Column 1. Since there is an error only in Column 2, the answer is A.

	Column 1	Column 2	Column 3	
16.	NEKKU	mytti	29987	16.____
17.	KRAEB	txyle	86095	17.____
18.	ENAUK	ymoit	92178	18.____
19.	REANA	xeomo	69121	19.____
20.	EKHSE	ytcxy	97049	20.____

Questions 21-30.

ARITHMETICAL REASONING

21. If a secretary answered 28 phone calls and typed the addresses for 112 credit statements in one morning, what is the ratio of phone calls answered to credit statements typed for that period of time?

    A. 1:4   B. 1:7   C. 2:3   D. 3:5

21.____

22. According to a suggested filing system, no more than 10 folders should be filed behind any one file guide and from 15 to 25 file guides should be used in each file drawer for easy finding and filing.
The maximum number of folders that a five-drawer file cabinet can hold to allow easy finding and filing is

    A. 550   B. 750   C. 1,100   D. 1,250

22.____

23. An employee had a starting salary of $25,804. He received a salary increase at the end of each year, and at the end of the seventh year his salary was $33,476.
What was his average annual increase in salary over these seven years?

    A. $1,020   B. $1,076   C. $1,096   D. $1,144

23.____

24. The 55 typists and 28 senior clerks in a certain city agency were paid a total of $1,943,200 in salaries last year.
If the average annual salary of a typist was $22,400 the average annual salary of a senior clerk was

    A. $25,400   B. $26,600   C. $26,800   D. $27,000

24.____

25. A typist has been given a three page report to type. She has finished typing the first two pages. The first page has 283 words, and the second page has 366 words.
If the total report consists of 954 words, how many words will she have to type on the third page of the report?

    A. 202   B. 287   C. 305   D. 313

25.____

26. In one day, Clerk A processed 30% more forms than Clerk B, and Clerk C processed Ii times as many forms as Clerk A. If Clerk B processed 40 forms, how many more forms were processed by Clerk C than Clerk B?

    A. 12   B. 13   C. 21   D. 25

26.____

27. A clerk who earns a gross salary of $452 every two weeks has the following deductions taken from her paycheck:
15% for City, State, Federal taxes; 2 1/2% for Social Security; $1.30 for health insurance; and $6.00 for union dues. The amount of her take-home pay is

    A. $256.20   B. $312.40   C. $331.60   D. $365.60

27.____

28. In 2005, a city agency spent $2,000 to buy pencils at a cost of $5.00 a dozen.
If the agency used 3/4 of these pencils in 2005 and used the same number of pencils in 2006, how many more pencils did it have to buy to have enough pencils for all of 2006?

    A. 1,200   B. 2,400   C. 3,600   D. 4,800

28.____

29. A clerk who worked in Agency X earned the following salaries: $20,140 the first year,$21,000 the second year, and $21,920 the third year. Another clerk who worked in Agency Y for three years earned $21,100 a year for two years and $21,448 the third year. The difference between the average salaries received by both clerks over a three-year period is

    A. $196   B. $204   C. $348   D. $564

29.____

30. An employee who works over 40 hours in any week receives overtime payment for the extra hours at time and one-half (1 1/2 times) his hourly rate of pay. An employee who earns $13.60 an hour works a total of 45 hours during a certain week.
His total pay for that week would be

    A. $564.40   B. $612.00   C. $646.00   D. $812.00

30.____

Questions 31-35.

RELATED INFORMATION

31. To tell a newly-employed clerk to fill a top drawer of a four-drawer cabinet with heavy folders which will be often used and to keep lower drawers only partly filled is

    A. *good,* because a tall person would have to bend unnecessarily if he had to use a lower drawer
    B. *bad,* because the file cabinet may tip over when the top drawer is opened
    C. *good,* because it is the most easily reachable drawer for the average person
    D. *bad,* because a person bending down at another drawer may accidentally bang his head on the bottom of the drawer when he straightens up

31.____

32. If a senior typist or senior clerk has requisitioned a *ream* of paper in order to duplicate a single page office announcement, how many announcements can be printed from the one package of paper?

    A. 200   B. 500   C. 700   D. 1,000

32.____

33. Your supervisor has asked you to locate a telephone number for an attorney named Jones, whose office is located at 311 Broadway, and whose name is not already listed in your files.
The BEST method for finding the number would be for you to

    A. call the information operator and have her get it for you
    B. look in the alphabetical directory (white pages) under the name Jones at 311 Broadway
    C. refer to the heading Attorney in the yellow pages for the name Jones at 311 Broadway
    D. ask your supervisor who referred her to Mr. Jones, then call that person for the number

33.____

34. An example of material that should NOT be sent by first class mail is a

    A. email copy of a letter   B. post card
    C. business reply card   D. large catalogue

34.____

35. In the operations of a government agency, a voucher is ORDINARILY used to   35._____

    A. refer someone to the agency for a position or assignment
    B. certify that an agency's records of financial trans-actions are accurate
    C. order payment from agency funds of a stated amount to an individual
    D. enter a statement of official opinion in the records of the agency

Questions 36-40.

ENGLISH USAGE

DIRECTIONS: Each question from 36 through 40 contains a sentence. Read each sentence carefully to decide whether it is correct. Then, in the space at the right, mark your answer:

    (A) if the sentence is incorrect because of bad grammar or sentence structure

    (B) if the sentence is incorrect because of bad punctuation

    (C) if the sentence is incorrect because of bad capitalization

    (D) if the sentence is correct

Each incorrect sentence has only one type of error. Consider a sentence correct if it has no errors, although there may be other correct ways of saying the same thing.

SAMPLE QUESTION I: One of our clerks were promoted yesterday.

The subject of this sentence is *one,* so the verb should be *was promoted* instead of *were promoted.* Since the sentence is incorrect because of bad grammar, the answer to Sample Question I is (A).

SAMPLE QUESTION II: Between you and me, I would prefer not going there.

Since this sentence is correct, the answer to Sample Question II is (D).

36. The National alliance of Businessmen is trying to persuade private businesses to hire youth in the summertime.   36._____

37. The supervisor who is on vacation, is in charge of processing vouchers.   37._____

38. The activity of the committee at its conferences is always stimulating.   38._____

39. After checking the addresses again, the letters went to the mailroom.   39._____

40. The director, as well as the employees, are interested in sharing the dividends.   40._____

Questions 41-45.

FILING

DIRECTIONS: Each question from 41 through 45 contains four names. For each question, choose the name that should be FIRST if the four names are to be arranged in alphabeti-cal order in accordance with the Rules for Alphabetical Filing given below. Read these rules carefully. Then, for each question, indicate in the space at the right the letter before the name that should be FIRST in alphabet-ical order.

RULES FOR ALPHABETICAL FILING

Names of People

(1)   The names of people are filed in strict alphabetical order, first according to the last name, then according to first name or initial, and finally according to middle name or initial. FOR EXAMPLE: George Allen comes before Edward Bell, and Leonard P. Reston comes before Lucille B. Reston.

(2)   When last names are the same, FOR EXAMPLE, A. Green and Agnes Green, the one with the initial comes before the one with the name written out when the first initials are identi-cal.

(3)   When first and last names are alike and the middle name is given, FOR EXAMPLE, John David Doe and John Devoe Doe, the names should be filed in the alphabetical order of the middle names.

(4)   When first and last names are the same, a name without a middle initial comes before one with a middle name or initial. FOR EXAMPLE, John Doe comes before both John A. Doe and John Alan Doe.

(5)   When first and last names are the same, a name with a middle initial comes before one with a middle name beginning with the same initial. FOR EXAMPLE: Jack R. Hertz comes before Jack Richard Hertz.

(6)   Prefixes such as De, O', Mac, Mc, and Van are filed as written and are treated as part of the names to which they are connected. FOR EXAMPLE: Robert O'Dea is filed before David Olsen.

(7)   Abbreviated names are treated as if they were spelled out. FOR EXAMPLE: Chas. is filed as Charles and Thos. is filed as Thomas.

(8)   Titles and designations such as Dr., Mr., and Prof, are disregarded in filing.

Names of Organizations

(1)   The names of business organizations are filed according to the order in which each word in the name appears. When an organization name bears the name of a person, it is filed according to the rules for filing names of people as given above. FOR EXAMPLE: William Smith Service Co. comes before Television Distributors, Inc.

(2) *Where bureau, board, office, or department appears as the first part of the title of a govern-mental agency, that agency should be filed under the word in the title expressing the chief function of the agency. FOR EXAMPLE: Bureau of the Budget would be filed as if written Budget, (Bureau of the). The Department of Personnel would be filed as if written Person-nel, (Department of).*

(3) *When the following words are part of an organization, they are disregarded: the, of, and.*

(4) *When there are numbers in a name, they are treated as if they were spelled out. FOR EXAMPLE: 10th Street Bootery is filed as Tenth Street Bootery.*

SAMPLE QUESTION:
A. Jane Earl   (2)
B. James A. Earle (4)
C. James Earl   (1)
D. J. Earle   (3)

The numbers in parentheses show the proper alphabetical order in which these names should be filed. Since the name that should be filed FIRST is James Earl, the answer to the Sample Question is (C).

41. A. Majorca Leather Goods
    B. Robert Maiorca and Sons
    C. Maintenance Management Corp.
    D. Majestic Carpet Mills

41._____

42. A. Municipal Telephone Service
    B. Municipal Reference Library
    C. Municipal Credit Union
    D. Municipal Broadcasting System

42._____

43. A. Robert B. Pierce   B. R. Bruce Pierce
    C. Ronald Pierce   D. Robert Bruce Pierce

43._____

44. A. Four Seasons Sports Club   B. 14th. St. Shopping Center
    C. Forty Thieves Restaurant   D. 42nd St. Theaters

44._____

45. A. Franco Franceschini   B. Amos Franchini
    C. Sandra Franceschia   D. Lilie Franchinesca

45._____

Questions 46-50.

SPELLING

DIRECTIONS: In each question, one of the words is misspelled. Select the letter of the mis-spelled word. *PRINT THE LETTER OF THE CORRECT ANSWER IN THE SPACE AT THE RIGHT.*

46. A. option   B. extradite
    C. comparitive   D. jealousy

46._____

47. A. handicaped   B. assurance
    C. sympathy   D. speech

47._____

48. A. recommend   B. carraige   48.____
     C. disapprove   D. independent

49. A. ingenuity   B. tenet (opinion)   49.____
     C. uncanny   D. intrigueing

50. A. arduous   B. hideous   50.____
     C. iervant   D. companies

KEY (CORRECT ANSWERS)

1.	A	11.	D	21.	A	31.	B	41.	C
2.	B	12.	B	22.	D	32.	B	42.	D
3.	D	13.	D	23.	C	33.	C	43.	B
4.	B	14.	B	24.	A	34.	D	44.	D
5.	D	15.	A	25.	C	35.	C	45.	C
6.	C	16.	B	26.	D	36.	C	46.	C
7.	A	17.	C	27.	D	37.	B	47.	A
8.	C	18.	D	28.	B	38.	D	48.	B
9.	D	19.	A	29.	A	39.	A	49.	D
10.	B	20.	C	30.	C	40.	A	50.	C'

EXAMINATION SECTION
TEST 1

DIRECTIONS: Each question or incomplete statement is followed by several suggested answers or completions. Select the one that BEST answers the question or completes the statement. *PRINT THE LETTER OF THE CORRECT ANSWER IN THE SPACE AT THE RIGHT.*

1. Which of the following is the acceptable format for typing the date line?   1.____

   A. 12/2/16   B. December 2, 2016
   C. December 2nd, 2016   D. Dec. 2 2016

2. When typing a letter, which of the following is INACCURATE?   2.____

   A. If the letter is to be more than one page long, subsequent sheets should be blank, but should match the letterhead sheet in size, color, weight, and texture.
   B. Long quoted material must be centered and single-spaced internally.
   C. Quotation marks must be used when there is long quoted material.
   D. Double spacing is used above and below tables and long quotations to set them off from the rest of the material.

3. Which of the following is INACCURATE?   3.____

   A. When an addressee's title in an inside address would overrun the center of a page, it's best to carry part of the title over to another line and to indent it by two spaces.
   B. It is permissible to use ordinal numbers in an inside address.
   C. In addresses involving street numbers under three, the number is written out in full.
   D. In the inside address, suite, apartment or room numbers should be placed on the line after the street address.

4. All of the following are common styles of business letters EXCEPT   4.____

   A. simplified   B. block
   C. direct   D. executive

5. Please select the two choices below that correctly represent how a continuation sheet heading may be typed.   5.____

   I.   Page 2   II. Page 2
        Mr. Alan Post   Mr. Alan Post
        June 25, 2016   6-25-16
   III. Mr. Alan Post   -2-   June 25, 2016
   IV. Mr. Alan Post   -2-   6-25-16

   The CORRECT answer is:

   A. I, II   B. II, III   C. I, III   D. II, IV

6. Which of the following is INCORRECT? It is   6.____

   A. permissible to abbreviate honorifics in the inside address
   B. permissible to abbreviate company or organizational names, departmental designations, or organizational titles in the inside address

C. permissible to use abbreviations in the inside address if they have been used on the printed letterhead and form part of the official company name
D. sometimes permissible to omit the colon after the salutation

7. Which of the following is INCORRECT?　　　　　　　　　　　　　　　7.____

   A. The subject line of a letter gives the main idea of the message as succinctly as possible.
   B. If a letter contains an enclosure, there should be a notation indicating this.
   C. Important enclosures ought to be listed numerically and described.
   D. An enclosure notation should be typed flush with the right margin.

8. Which of the following is INACCURATE about inside addresses?　　　　8.____

   A. An intraoffice or intracompany mail stop number such as DA 3C 61B is put after the organization or company name with at least two spaces intervening.
   B. Words such as *Avenue* should not be abbreviated.
   C. With the exception of runovers, the inside address should not be more than five full lines.
   D. The inside address includes the recipient's courtesy or honorific title and his or her full name on line one; the recipient's title on the next line; the recipient's official organizational affiliation on the next line; the street address on the penultimate line; and the city, state, and zip code on the last line.

9. Which of the following is an INCORRECT example of how to copy recipients when using copy notation?　　　　　　　　　　　　　　　　　　　　　　　9.____

   A. cc: Martin A.Sheen　　　　　　　B. cc:　Ms. Connors
   　　　　　　　　　　　　　　　　　　　　　　　Ms. Grogan
   　　　　　　　　　　　　　　　　　　　　　　　Ms. Reynolds
   C. CC: Martin A. Sheen　　　　　　D. cc:　Mr. Right
   　　　　　　　　　　　　　　　　　　　　　　　Mr. Wrong
   　　　　　　　　　　　　　　　　　　　　　　　Mr. Perfect

10. When typing a memo, all of the following are true EXCEPT　　　　　10.____

   A. it is permissible to use an abbreviation like 1/1/16
   B. the subject line should be underlined
   C. titles such as *Mr.* or *Dr.* are usually not used on the *To* line
   D. unless the memo is very short, paragraphs should be single-spaced and double spacing should be used to separate the paragraphs from each other

11. When typing a letter, which of the following is INACCURATE?　　　11.____

   A. Paragraphs in business letters are usually single-spaced, with double spacing separating them from each other.
   B. Margin settings used on subsequent sheets should match those used on the letterhead sheet.
   C. If the message contains an enumerated list, it is best to block and center the listed material by five or six more spaces, right and left.
   D. A quotation of more than three typed lines must be single-spaced and centered on the page.

12. A letter that is to be signed by Hazel Alice Putney, but written by Mary Jane Roberts, and typed by Alice Carol Bell would CORRECTLY bear the following set of initials:

    A. HAP:MJR:acb   B. HAP:MJR:ab
    C. HAP:mjr:acb   D. HAP:mjr:ab

12.____

13. Which of the following is INCORRECT?

    A. My dear Dr. Jones:
    B. Dear Accounting Department:
    C. Dear Dr. Jones:
    D. Dear Mr. Al Lee, Esq.:

13.____

14. Which of the following is INCORRECT?

    A. Bcc stands for blind copy or blind courtesy copy.
    B. When a blind copy is used, the notation bcc appears only on the original.
    C. When a blind copy is used, the notation may appear in the top left corner of the letterhead sheet.
    D. If following a letter style that uses indented paragraphs, the postscript should be indented in exactly the same manner.

14.____

15. All of the following are true of the complimentary close EXCEPT

    A. it is typed two lines beneath the last line of the message
    B. when using a minimal punctuation system, you may omit the comma in the complimentary close if you have used a colon in the salutation
    C. where the complimentary close is placed may vary
    D. the first word of the complimentary close is capitalized

15.____

16. When typing a letter, which of the following is INACCURATE?

    A. Tables should be centered.
    B. If the letter is to be more than one page long, at least three lines of the message itself should be carried over.
    C. The message begins two lines below the salutation in almost all letter styles.
    D. Triple spacing should be used above and below lists to set them off from the rest of the letter.

16.____

17. Which one of the following is INCORRECT?

    A. When used, special mailing instructions should be indicated on both the envelope and the letter itself.
    B. Depending upon the length of the message and the available space, special mailing instructions are usually typed flush left, about four spaces below the date line and about two lines above the first line of the inside address.
    C. Certification, registration, special delivery, and overseas air mail are all considered special mailing instructions.
    D. Special mailing instructions should not be typed in capital letters.

17.____

18. Which of the following is INCORRECT?

    A. When a letter is intended to be personal or confidential, these instructions are typewritten in capital letters on the envelope and on the letter itself.

18.____

4 (#1)

B. When a letter is intended to be personal or confidential, these instructions are type-written in capital letters on the envelope, but not on the letter.
C. A letter marked PERSONAL is an eyes-only communication for the recipient.
D. A letter marked CONFIDENTIAL means that the recipient and any other authorized person may open and read it.

19. All of the following are true in regard to copy notation EXCEPT   19._____

   A. when included in a letter, a copy notation should be typed flush with the left margin, two lines below the signature block or two lines below any preceding notation
   B. copy notation should appear after writer/typist initials and/or enclosure notations, if these are used
   C. the copy recipient's full name and address should be indicated
   D. if more than one individual is to be copied, recipients should be listed in alphabetical order according to full name or initials

20. When addressing envelopes, which of the following is INACCURATE?   20._____

   A. When both street address and box number are used, the destination of the letter should be placed on the line just above the city, state, and zip code line.
   B. Special mailing instructions are typed in capital letters below the postage.
   C. Special handling instructions should be typed in capital letters and underlined.
   D. The address should be single-spaced.

21. All of the following should be capitalized EXCEPT the   21._____

   A. first word of a direct quotation
   B. first word in the continuation of a split, single-sentence quotation
   C. names of organizations
   D. names of places and geographic districts, regions, divisions, and locales

22. All of the following are true about capitalization EXCEPT   22._____

   A. words indicating direction and regions are capitalized
   B. the names of rivers, seas, lakes, mountains, and oceans are capitalized
   C. the names of nationalities, tribes, languages, and races are capitalized
   D. civil, military, corporate, royal and noble, honorary, and religious titles are capitalized when they precede a name

23. All of the following are true about capitalization EXCEPT   23._____

   A. key words in the titles of musical, dramatic, artistic, and literary works are capitalized as are the first and last words
   B. the first word of the salutation and of the complimentary close of a letter is capitalized
   C. abbreviations and acronyms are not capitalized
   D. the days of the week, months of the year, holidays, and holy days are capitalized

24. All of the following are true EXCEPT   24._____

   A. an apostrophe indicates the omission of letters in contractions
   B. an apostrophe indicates the possessive case of singular and plural nouns

72

C. an apostrophe should not be used to indicate the omission of figures in dates
D. ellipses are used to indicate the omission of words or sentences within quoted material

25. All of the following are true EXCEPT   25.____

   A. brackets may be used to enclose words or passages in quotations to indicate the insertion of material written by someone other than the original writer
   B. brackets may be used to enclose material that is inserted within material already in parentheses
   C. a dash, rather than a colon, should be used to introduce a list
   D. a colon may be used to introduce a long quotation

26. All of the following are true EXCEPT a(n)   26.____

   A. comma may be used to set off short quotations and sayings
   B. apostrophe is often used to represent the word *per*
   C. dash may be used to indicate a sudden change or break in continuity
   D. dash may be used to set apart an emphatic or defining phrase

27. All of the following are true EXCEPT   27.____

   A. a hyphen may be used as a substitute for the word *to* between figures or words
   B. parentheses are used to enclose material that is not an essential part of the sentence and that, if not included, would not change its meaning
   C. single quotation marks are used to enclose quotations within quotations
   D. semicolons and colons are put inside closing quotation marks

28. All of the following are true EXCEPT   28.____

   A. commas and periods should be put inside closing quotation marks
   B. for dramatic effect, a semicolon may be used instead of a comma to signal longer pauses
   C. a semicolon is used to set off city and state in geographic names
   D. italics are used to represent the titles of magazines and newspapers

29. According to standard rules for typing, two spaces are left after a   29.____

   A. closing parenthesis   B. comma
   C. number   D. colon

30. All of the following are true EXCEPT   30.____

   A. rounding out large numbers is often acceptable
   B. it is best to use numerical figures to express specific hours, measures, dates, page numbers, coordinates, and addresses
   C. when a sentence begins with a number, it is best to use numerical figures rather than to spell the number out
   D. when two or more numbers appear in one sentence, it is best to spell them out consistently or use numerical figures consistently, regardless of the size of the numbers

31. All of the following are true about word division EXCEPT   31.____

    A. words should not be divided on a single letter
    B. it is acceptable to carry over two-letter endings
    C. the final word in a paragraph should not be divided
    D. words in headings should not be divided

32. All of the following are true of word division EXCEPT   32.____

    A. it is preferable to divide words of three or more syllables after the consonant
    B. it is best to avoid breaking words on more than two consecutive lines
    C. words should be divided according to pronunciation
    D. two-syllable words are divided at the end of the first syllable

33. All of the following are true of word division EXCEPT   33.____

    A. words with short prefixes should be divided after the prefix
    B. prefixes and combining forms of more than one syllable should be divided after the first syllable
    C. the following word endings are not divided: -gion, -gious, -sial, -sion, -tial, -tion, -tious, -ceous, -cial, -cient, -cion, -cious, and -geous
    D. words ending in -er should not be divided if the division could only occur on the -er form

34. All of the following are true about word division EXCEPT   34.____

    A. words should be divided so that the part of the word left at the end of the line will suggest the word
    B. abbreviations should not be divided
    C. the suffixes -able and -ible are usually divided instead of being carried over intact to the next line
    D. when the addition of -ed, -est, -er, or a similar ending causes the doubling of a final consonant, the added consonant is carried over

35. All of the following are true of word division EXCEPT   35.____

    A. words with doubled consonants are usually divided between those consonants
    B. it is permissible to divide contractions
    C. words of one syllable should not be split
    D. it is best to try to avoid divisions that add a hyphen to an already hyphenated word

36. All of the following are true of word division EXCEPT   36.____

    A. dividing proper names should be avoided wherever possible
    B. two consonants, preceded and followed by a vowel, are divided after the first consonant
    C. even though two adjoining vowels are sounded separately, it is best not to divide between the two vowels
    D. it is best not to divide the month and day when typing dates, but the year may be carried over to the next line

37. Which of the following four statements are CORRECT? It would be acceptable to divide the word
    I.   *organization* after the first *a* in the word
    II. *recommend* after the first *m*
    III. *interface* between the *r* and the *f*
    IV. *development* between the *e* and the *l*
    The CORRECT answer is:

    A. I *only*   B. II, III
    C. II *only*   D. I, II, III

    37.____

38. Which of the following is divided INCORRECTLY?

    A. usu-ally   B. call-ing
    C. pro-blem   D. micro-computer

    38.____

39. Which of the following is divided INCORRECTLY?

    A. imag-inary   B. commun-ity
    C. manage-able   D. commun-ion

    39.____

40. Which of the following is divided INCORRECTLY?

    A. spa-ghetti   B. retro-spective
    C. proof-reader   D. fix-ed

    40.____

41. Which of the following is divided INCORRECTLY?

    A. Mr. Han-rahan   B. control-lable
    C. pro-jectile   D. proj-ect

    41.____

42. Which of the following is divided INCORRECTLY?

    A. prom-ise   B. han-dling
    C. have-n't   D. pro-duce

    42.____

43. Which of the following is divided INCORRECTLY?

    A. ship-ped   B. audi-ble
    C. hypo-crite   D. refer-ring

    43.____

44. Which of the following is divided INCORRECTLY?

    A. particu-lar   B. spac-ious
    C. chang-ing   D. capac-ity

    44.____

45. There is a critical need to develop the ability to control the mind, especailly the ability to stop repeating negative thoughts. Often, when we must swallow our anger, we are left running an enless tape of thoughts. We can't stop thinking about what the person said and what we should have said in response. To combat this tendency, it is helpful to practice witnessing our thoughts. If we can remain detached from them, we won't fuel them, and they will just run out of gas. As we watch them, we also learn a lot about ourselves. The catch here is not to judge them. Judging may lead to selfblaming, blaming others, excuses, rationalizations, and other thoughts that just add fuel. Another technique is is substituting positive thoughts for negative ones.

    45.____

It is difficult to do this in the "heat of the moment". With practice, however, its possible
to train the mind to do what we want it to do and to contain what we want it to contain.
A mind is like a garden – we can weed it, or we can let it grow wild.
The above paragraph contains a number of typographical errors.
How many lines in this paragraph contain typographical errors?

A. 5 B. 6 C. 8 D. 9

KEY (CORRECT ANSWERS)

1.	B	11.	D	21.	B	31.	B	41.	A
2.	C	12.	A	22.	A	32.	A	42.	A
3.	D	13.	D	23.	C	33.	B	43.	A
4.	C	14.	B	24.	C	34.	C	44.	B
5.	C	15.	B	25.	C	35.	B	45.	C
6.	B	16.	D	26.	B	36.	C		
7.	D	17.	D	27.	D	37.	B		
8.	B	18.	B	28.	C	38.	C		
9.	D	19.	C	29.	D	39.	B		
10.	B	20.	C	30.	C	40.	D		

TEST 2

DIRECTIONS: Each sentence may or may not contain problems in capitalization or punctuation. If there is an error, select the number of the underlined part that must be changed to make the sentence correct. If the sentence has no error, select choice E. No sentence contains more than one error.

1. Is the choice for President of the company George Dawson or Marilyn Kappel ?
    A   B   C   D
    No error
    E

1. _____

2. "To tell you the truth , I was really disappointed that our Fall percentages did not show
    A   B   C
    more sales growth , " remarked the bookkeeper.   No error
    D   E

2. _____

3. Bruce gave his Uncle clear directions to go south on Maplewood Drive turn left at the
    A   B   C
    intersection with Birch Lane, and then proceed for two miles until he reached Columbia
    County . No error
    D   E

3. _____

4. Janet hopes to transfer to a college in the east during her junior year. No error
    A   B   C   D   E

4. _____

5. The Declaration of Independence states that we have the right to the pursuit of
    A   B   C
    Happiness , but it doesn't guarantee that we'll ever find it.   No error
    D   E

5. _____

6. We campaigned hard for the mayor, but we ' re still not sure if he'll win against Senator
    A   B   C   D
    Frankovich. No error
    E

6. _____

7. Mr. Butler ' s Ford was parked right behind our's on Atlantic Avenue . No error
    A   B   C   D   E

7. _____

8. "I respect your opinion, but I cannot agree with it . " commented my grandmother.
    A   B   C   D
    No error
    E

8. _____

9. My friends‚ of course‚ were surprised ‗when when I did so well on the Math section
         A   B   C   D

    of the test. No error
                  E

9.____

10. Dr. Vogel and Senator Rydell decided ‗that the meeting would be held on February 6‚
               A   B   C

    in Ithaca‚ New York. No error
          D   E

10.____

11. "Frank‗ do you understand what we're telling you?" asked the doctor. No error
       A   B   C   D   E

11.____

12. When I asked my daughter what she knew about politics‗ she claimed‗she
                 A   B   C

    knew nothing. No error
          D   E

12.____

13. "If you went to my high school‚ dad, you' d see things differently," snapped Sean.
                 A   A   B C   D

    No error
       E

13.____

14. In Carlos' third year of high school, he took geometry, psychology, french, and chemis-
        A   B   B   C   D

    try. No error
          E

14.____

15. "When you enter the building‚" the guard instructed us‚ "turn left down the long‚ wind-
                     A   B C   D

    ing corridor." No error
              E

15.____

16. We hope to spend a weekend in the Catskill Mountains in the spring‚ and we' d like to
                                   A   B   C   D

    go to Florida in January. No error
                     E

16.____

17. A clerk in the department of Justice asked Carol and me if we were there on business or
      A   B   C

    just sight- seeing‚ . No error
            D   E

17.____

18. Jamie joined a cult, Harry's in a rock band, and Carol-Ann is studying chinese literature
   A   B   C

   at the University of Southern California. No error
            D   E

18.____

19. Parker Flash asked if my band had ever played at the
                   A

   Purple Turnip, a club in Orinoco Hills . No error
   B   C   D   E

19.____

20. "The gift of the Magi" is a short story by O'Henry that deals with the sad ironies of life.
        A B C D

   No error
       E

20.____

21. Darwin's theory was developed, as a result of his trip to the Galapagos Islands. ·
        A B   C   D

   No error
       E

21.____

22. Is 10 Downing street the address of Sherlock Holmes or the British Prime Minister ?
        A   B   C   D

   No error
       E

22.____

23. While President Johnson was in Office, his Great Society program passed a great deal
           A   B   C   D   D

   of important legislation. No error
                              E

23.____

24. If, as the American Industrial Health Council 's study says, one out of every five can-
    A   B   C

   cers today is caused by the workplace, it is a tragic indictment of what is happening
                              D

   there. No error
            E

24.____

25. According to the Articles of Confederation, Congress could issue money, but it could
                              A   B   C

   not prevent States from issuing their own money. No error
                  D   E

25.____

26. "I'd really like to know whos going to be shoveling the driveway this winter," said
                 A B   C   D

    Laverne. No error
                  E

    26.____

27. According to Carl Jung the Swiss psychologist, playing with fantasy is the key to cre-
                         A   B   C   D

    ativity. No error
               E

    27.____

28. Don't you find it odd that people would prefer jumping A off the Golden Gate bridge to
      A   B

    jumping off other bridges in the area? No error
                          C D   E

    28.____

29. While driving through the South, we saw many of the sites of famous Civil war battles. .
                        A   B   C D

    No error
      E

    29.____

30. Although I have always valued my Grandmother's china, I prefer her collection
                                  A   B C

    of South American art. No error
       D   E

    30.____

KEY (CORRECT ANSWERS)

1.	A		16.	E
2.	C		17.	B
3.	A		18.	C
4.	B		19.	C
5.	D		20.	A
6.	E		21.	C
7.	C		22.	B
8.	E		23.	B
9.	D		24.	D
10.	E		25.	D
11.	A		26.	B
12.	B		27.	A
13.	C		28.	B
14.	D		29.	C
15.	E		30.	A

———

READING COMPREHENSION
UNDERSTANDING AND INTERPRETING WRITTEN MATERIAL
EXAMINATION SECTION
TEST 1

DIRECTIONS: Each question or incomplete statement is followed by several suggested answers or completions. Select the one that BEST answers the question or completes the statement. *PRINT THE LETTER OF THE CORRECT ANSWER IN THE SPACE AT THE RIGHT.*

Questions 1-3.

DIRECTIONS: Questions 1 through 3 are to be answered SOLELY on the basis of the following paragraph.

Every organization needs a systematic method of checking its operations as a means to increase efficiency and promote economy. Many successful private firms have instituted a system of audits or internal inspections to accomplish these ends. Law enforcement organizations, which have an extremely important service to *sell,* should be no less zealous in developing efficiency and economy in their operations. Periodic, organized, and systematic inspections are one means of promoting the achievement of these objectives. The necessity of an organized inspection system is perhaps greatest in those law enforcement groups which have grown to such a size that the principal officer can no longer personally supervise or be cognizant of every action taken. Smooth and effective operation demands that the head of the organization have at hand some tool with which he can study and enforce general policies and procedures and also direct compliance with day-to-day orders, most of which are put into execution outside his sight and hearing. A good inspection system can serve as that tool.

1. The central thought of the above paragraph is that a system of inspections within a police department

    A. is unnecessary for a department in which the principal officer can personally supervise all official actions taken
    B. should be instituted at the first indication that there is any deterioration in job performance by the force
    C. should be decentralized and administered by first-line supervisory officers
    D. is an important aid to the police administrator in the accomplishment of law enforcement objectives

1.____

2. The MOST accurate of the following statements concerning the need for an organized inspection system in a law enforcement organization is: It is

    A. never needed in an organization of small size where the principal officer can give personal supervision
    B. most needed where the size of the organization prevents direct supervision by the principal officer
    C. more needed in law enforcement organizations than in private firms
    D. especially needed in an organization about to embark upon a needed expansion of services

2.____

3. According to the above paragraph, the head of the police organization utilizes the internal inspection system   3.____

    A. as a tool which must be constantly re-examined in the light of changing demands for police service
    B. as an administrative technique to increase efficiency and promote economy
    C. by personally visiting those areas of police operation which are outside his sight and hearing
    D. to augment the control of local commanders over detailed field operations

Questions 4-10.

DIRECTIONS: Questions 4 through 10 are to be answered SOLELY on the basis of the following passage.

Job evaluation and job rating systems are intended to introduce scientific procedures. Any type of approach, when properly used, will give satisfactory results. The Point System, when properly validated by actual use, is more likely to be suitable for general use than the ranking system. In many aspects, the Factor Comparison Plan is a point system tied to money values. Of course, there may be another system that combines the ranking system with the point system, especially during the initial stages of the development of the program. After the program has been in use for some time, the tendency is to drop off the ranking phase and continue the use of the point system.

In the ranking system of rating of jobs, every job within the plant is arranged in some order, either from the one with the simplest qualifications to the one with maximum requirements, or in the reverse order. This system should be preceded by careful job analysis and the writing of accurate job descriptions before the rating process is undertaken. It is possible, of course, to take the jobs as they are found in the business enterprise and use the names as they are without any attempt at standardization, and merely rank them according to the general over-all impression of the raters. Such a procedure is certain to fall short of what may reasonably be expected of job rating. Another procedure that is in reality merely a modification of the simple rating described above is to establish a series of grades or zones and arrange all the jobs in the plant into groups within these grades and zones. The practice in most common use is to arrange all the jobs in the plant according to their requirements by rating them and then to establish the classifications or groups.

The actual ranking of jobs may be done by one individual, several individuals, or a committee. If several individuals are working independently on the task, it will usually be found that, in general, they agree but that their rankings vary in certain details. A conference between the individuals, with each person giving his reasons why he rated one way or another, usually produces agreement. The detailed job descriptions are particularly helpful when there is disagreement among raters as to the rating of certain jobs. It is not only possible but desirable to have workers participate in the construction of the job description and in rating the job.

4. The MAIN theme of this passage is   4.____

    A. the elimination of bias in job rating
    B. the rating of jobs by the ranking system

C. the need for accuracy in allocating points in the point system
D. pitfalls to avoid in selecting key jobs in the Factor Comparison Plan

5. The ranking system of rating jobs consists MAINLY of 5.____

A. attaching a point value to each ratable factor of each job prior to establishing an equitable pay scale
B. arranging every job in the organization in descending order and then following this up with a job analysis of the key jobs
C. preparing accurate job descriptions after a job analysis and then arranging all jobs either in ascending or descending order based on job requirements
D. arbitrarily establishing a hierarchy of job classes and grades and then fitting each job into a specific class and grade based on the opinions of unit supervisors

6. The above passage states that the system of classifying jobs MOST used in an organiza- 6.____
tion is to

A. organize all jobs in the organization in accordance with their requirements and then create categories or clusters of jobs
B. classify all jobs in the organization according to the titles and rank by which they are currently known in the organization
C. establish a pre-arranged series of grades or zones and then fit
D. all jobs into one of the grades or zones
E. determine the salary currently being paid for each job and then rank the jobs in order according to salary

7. According to the above passage, experience has shown that when a group of raters is 7.____
assigned to the job evaluation task and each individual rates independently of the others,
the raters GENERALLY

A. agree with respect to all aspects of their rankings
B. disagree with respect to all or nearly all aspects of the rankings
C. disagree on overall ratings, but agree on specific rating factors
D. agree on overall rankings, but have some variance in some details

8. The above passage states that the use of a detailed job description is of SPECIAL value 8.____
when

A. employees of an organization have participated in the preliminary step involved in actual preparation of the job description
B. labor representatives are not participating in ranking of the jobs
C. an individual rater who is unsure of himself is ranking the jobs
D. a group of raters is having difficulty reaching unanimity with respect to ranking a certain job

9. A comparison of the various rating systems as described in the above passage shows 9.____
that

A. the ranking system is not as appropriate for general use as a properly validated point system
B. the point system is the same as the Factor Comparison Plan except that it places greater emphasis on money

    C.   no system is capable of combining the point system and the Factor Comparison
        Plan
    D.   the point system will be discontinued last when used in combination with the Factor
        Comparison System

10.   The above passage implies that the PRINCIPAL reason for creating job evaluation and   10.____
     rating systems was to help

    A.   overcome union opposition to existing salary plans
    B.   base wage determination on a more objective and orderly foundation
    C.   eliminate personal bias on the part of the trained scientific job evaluators
    D.   management determine if it was overpricing the various jobs in the organizational
        hierarchy

Questions 11-13.

DIRECTIONS: Questions 11 through 13 are to be answered SOLELY on the basis of the fol-
                lowing paragraph.

The common sense character of the merit system seems so natural to most Americans
that many people wonder why it should ever have been inoperative. After all, the American
economic system, the most phenomenal the world has ever known, is also founded on a rug-
ged selective process which emphasizes the personal qualities of capacity, industriousness,
and productivity. The criteria may not have always been appropriate and competition has not
always been fair, but competition there was, and the responsibilities and the rewards – with
exceptions, of course – have gone to those who could measure up in terms of intelligence,
knowledge, or perseverance. This has been true not only in the economic area, in the money-
making process, but also in achievement in the professions and other walks of life.

11.   According to the above paragraph, economic rewards in the United States have   11.____

    A.   always been based on appropriate, fair criteria
    B.   only recently been based on a competitive system
    C.   not gone to people who compete too ruggedly
    D.   usually gone to those people with intelligence, knowledge, and perseverance

12.   According to the above passage, a merit system is   12.____

    A.   an unfair criterion on which to base rewards
    B.   unnatural to anyone who is not American
    C.   based only on common sense
    D.   based on the same principles as the American economic system

13.   According to the above passage, it is MOST accurate to say that   13.____

    A.   the United States has always had a civil service merit system
    B.   civil service employees are very rugged
    C.   the American economic system has always been based on a merit objective
    D.   competition is unique to the American way of life

Questions 14-15.

DIRECTIONS: Questions 14 and 15 are to be answered SOLELY on the basis of the following paragraph.

In-basket tests are often used to assess managerial potential. The exercise consists of a set of papers that would be likely to be found in the in-basket of an administrator or manager at any given time, and requires the individuals participating in the examination to indicate how they would dispose of each item found in the in-basket. In order to handle the in-basket effectively, they must successfully manage their time, refer and assign some work to subordinates, juggle potentially conflicting appointments and meetings, and arrange for follow-up of problems generated by the items in the in-basket. In other words, the in-basket test is attempting to evaluate the participants' abilities to organize their work, set priorities, delegate, control, and make decisions.

14.   According to the above paragraph, to succeed in an in-basket test, an administrator must   14._____

    A.   be able to read very quickly
    B.   have a great deal of technical knowledge
    C.   know when to delegate work
    D.   arrange a lot of appointments and meetings

15.   According to the above paragraph, all of the following abilities are indications of manage-   15._____
rial potential EXCEPT the ability to

    A.   organize and control   B.   manage time
    C.   write effective reports   D.   make appropriate decisions

Questions 16-19.

DIRECTIONS: Questions 16 through 19 are to be answered SOLELY on the basis of the following paragraph.

A personnel researcher has at his disposal various approaches for obtaining information, analyzing it, and arriving at conclusions that have value in predicting and affecting the behavior of people at work. The type of method to be used depends on such factors as the nature of the research problem, the available data, and the attitudes of those people being studied to the various kinds of approaches. While the experimental approach, with its use of control groups, is the most refined type of study, there are others that are often found useful in personnel research. Surveys, in which the researcher obtains facts on a problem from a variety of sources, are employed in research on wages, fringe benefits, and labor relations. Historical studies are used to trace the development of problems in order to understand them better and to isolate possible causative factors. Case studies are generally developed to explore all the details of a particular problem that is representative of other similar problems. A researcher chooses the most appropriate form of study for the problem he is investigating. He should recognize, however, that the experimental method, commonly referred to as the scientific method, if used validly and reliably, gives the most conclusive results.

16.   The above paragraph discusses several approaches used to obtain information on par-   16._____
ticular problems. Which of the following may be MOST reasonably concluded from the paragraph?
A(n)

A. historical study cannot determine causative factors
B. survey is often used in research on fringe benefits
C. case study is usually used to explore a problem that is unique and unrelated to other problems
D. experimental study is used when the scientific approach to a problem fails

17. According to the above paragraph, all of the following are factors that may determine the type of approach a researcher uses EXCEPT   17.____

    A. the attitudes of people toward being used in control groups
    B. the number of available sources
    C. his desire to isolate possible causative factors
    D. the degree of accuracy he requires

18. The words *scientific method*, as used in the last sentence of the above paragraph, refer to a type of study which, according to the above paragraph   18.____

    A. uses a variety of sources
    B. traces the development of problems
    C. uses control groups
    D. analyzes the details of a representative problem

19. Which of the following can be MOST reasonably concluded from the above paragraph? In obtaining and analyzing information on a particular problem, a researcher employs the method which is the   19.____

    A. most accurate   B. most suitable
    C. least expensive   D. least time-consuming

Questions 20-25.

DIRECTIONS: Questions 20 through 25 are to be answered SOLELY on the basis of the following passage.

The quality of the voice of a worker is an important factor in conveying to clients and co-workers his attitude and, to some degree, his character. The human voice, when not consciously disguised, may reflect a person's mood, temper, and personality. It has been shown in several experiments that certain character traits can be assessed with better than chance accuracy through listening to the voice of an unknown person who cannot be seen.

Since one of the objectives of the worker is to put clients at ease and to present an encouraging and comfortable atmosphere, a harsh, shrill, or loud voice could have a negative effect. A client who displays emotions of anger or resentment would probably be provoked even further by a caustic tone. In a face-to-face situation, an unpleasant voice may be compensated for, to some degree, by a concerned and kind facial expression. However, when one speaks on the telephone, the expression on one's face cannot be seen by the listener. A supervising clerk who wishes to represent himself effectively to clients should try to eliminate as many faults as possible in striving to develop desirable voice qualities.

20. If a worker uses a sarcastic tone while interviewing a resentful client, the client, according to the above passage, would MOST likely

    A. avoid the face-to-face situation
    B. be ashamed of his behavior
    C. become more resentful
    D. be provoked to violence

20._____

21. According to the passage, experiments comparing voice and character traits have demonstrated that

    A. prospects for improving an unpleasant voice through training are better than chance
    B. the voice can be altered to project many different psychological characteristics
    C. the quality of the human voice reveals more about the speaker than his words do
    D. the speaker's voice tells the hearer something about the speaker's personality

21._____

22. Which of the following, according to the above passage, is a person's voice MOST likely to reveal?
His

    A. prejudices   B. intelligence
    C. social awareness   D. temperament

22._____

23. It may be MOST reasonably concluded from the above passage that an interested and sympathetic expression on the face of a worker

    A. may induce a client to feel certain he will receive welfare benefits
    B. will eliminate the need for pleasant vocal qualities in the interviewer
    C. may help to make up for an unpleasant voice in the interviewer
    D. is desirable as the interviewer speaks on the telephone to a client

23._____

24. Of the following, the MOST reasonable implication of the above paragraph is that a worker should, when speaking to a client, control and use his voice to

    A. simulate a feeling of interest in the problems of the client
    B. express his emotions directly and adequately
    C. help produce in the client a sense of comfort and security
    D. reflect his own true personality

24._____

25. It may be concluded from the above passage that the PARTICULAR reason for a worker to pay special attention to modulating her voice when talking on the phone to a client is that, during a telephone conversation,

    A. there is a necessity to compensate for the way in which a telephone distorts the voice
    B. the voice of the worker is a reflection of her mood and character
    C. the client can react only on the basis of the voice and words she hears
    D. the client may have difficulty getting a clear under-standing over the telephone

25._____

KEY (CORRECT ANSWERS)

1.	D	11.	D
2.	B	12.	D
3.	B	13.	C
4.	B	14.	C
5.	C	15.	C
6.	A	16.	B
7.	D	17.	D
8.	D	18.	C
9.	A	19.	B
10.	B	20.	C

21. D
22. D
23. C
24. C
25. C

TEST 2

Questions 1-3.

DIRECTIONS: Questions 1 through 3 are to be answered SOLELY on the basis of the following paragraph.

Suppose you are given the job of printing, collating, and stapling 8,000 copies of a ten-page booklet as soon as possible. You have available one photo-offset machine, a collator with an automatic stapler, and the personnel to operate these machines. All will be available for however long the job takes to complete. The photo-offset machine prints 5,000 impressions an hour, and it takes about 15 minutes to set up a plate. The collator, including time for insertion of pages and stapling, can process about 2,000 booklets an hour. (Answers should be based on the assumption that there are no breakdowns or delays.)

1. Assuming that all the printing is finished before the collating is started, if the job is given to you late Monday and your section can begin work the next day and is able to devote seven hours a day, Monday through Friday, to the job until it is finished, what is the BEST estimate of when the job will be finished?

    1.____

    A. Wednesday afternoon of the same week
    B. Thursday morning of the same week
    C. Friday morning of the same week
    D. Monday morning of the next week

2. An operator suggests to you that instead of completing all the printing and then beginning collating and stapling, you first print all the pages for 4,000 booklets, so that they can be collated and stapled while the last 4,000 booklets are being printed.
If you accepted this suggestion, the job would be completed

    2.____

    A. sooner but would require more man-hours
    B. at the same time using either method
    C. later and would require more man-hours
    D. sooner but there would be more wear and tear on the plates

3. Assume that you have the same assignment and equipment as described above, but 16,000 copies of the booklet are needed instead of 8,000.
If you decided to print 8,000 complete booklets, then collate and staple them while you started printing the next 8,000 booklets, which of the following statements would MOST accurately describe the relationship between this new method and your original method of printing all the booklets at one time, and then collating and stapling them?
The

    3.____

    A. job would be completed at the same time regardless of the method used
    B. new method would result in the job's being completed 3 1/2 hours earlier
    C. original method would result in the job's being completed an hour later
    D. new method would result in the job's being completed 1 1/2 hours earlier.

Questions 4-6.

DIRECTIONS: Questions 4 through 6 are to be answered SOLELY on the basis of the following passage.

When using words like company, association, council, committee, and board in place of the full official name, the writer should not capitalize these short forms unless he intends them to invoke the full force of the institution's authority. In legal contracts, in minutes, or in formal correspondence where one is speaking formally and officially on behalf of the company, the term Company is usually capitalized, but in ordinary usage, where it is not essential to load the short form with this significance, capitalization would be excessive. (Example: The company will have many good openings for graduates this June.)

The treatment recommended for short forms of place names is essentially the same as that recommended for short forms of organizational names. In general, we capitalize the full form but not the short form. If Park Avenue is referred to in one sentence, then the *avenue* is sufficient in subsequent references. The same is true with words like building, hotel, station, and airport, which are capitalized when part of a proper name changed (Pan Am Building, Hotel Plaza, Union Station, O'Hare Airport), but are simply lower-cased when replacing these specific names.

4. The above passage states that USUALLY the short forms of names of organizations   4.____

   A. and places should not be capitalized
   B. and places should be capitalized
   C. should not be capitalized, but the short forms of names of places should be capitalized
   D. should be capitalized, but the short forms of names of places should not be capitalized

5. The above passage states that in legal contracts, in minutes, and in formal correspondence, the short forms of names of organizations should   5.____

   A. usually not be capitalized
   B. usually be capitalized
   C. usually not be used
   D. never be used

6. It can be INFERRED from the above passage that decisions regarding when to capitalize certain words   6.____

   A. should be left to the discretion of the writer
   B. should be based on generally accepted rules
   C. depend on the total number of words capitalized
   D. are of minor importance

Questions 7-10.

DIRECTIONS: Questions 7 through 10 are to be answered SOLELY on the basis of the following passage.

Use of the systems and procedures approach to office management is revolutionizing the supervision of office work. This approach views an enterprise as an entity which seeks to fulfill definite objectives. Systems and procedures help to organize repetitive work into a routine, thus reducing the amount of decision making required for its accomplishment. As a result, employees are guided in their efforts and perform only necessary work. Supervisors are relieved of any details of execution and are free to attend to more important work. Establishing work guides which require that identical tasks be performed the same way each time permits standardization of forms, machine operations, work methods, and controls. This approach also reduces the probability of errors. Any error committed is usually discovered quickly because the incorrect work does not meet the requirement of the work guides. Errors are also reduced through work specialization, which allows each employee to become thoroughly proficient in a particular type of work. Such proficiency also tends to improve the morale of the employees.

7. The above passage states that the accuracy of an employee's work is INCREASED by   7._____

    A. using the work specialization approach
    B. employing a probability sample
    C. requiring him to shift at one time into different types of tasks
    D. having his supervisor check each detail of work execution

8. Of the following, which one BEST expresses the main theme of the above passage? The   8._____

    A. advantages and disadvantages of the systems and procedures approach to office management
    B. effectiveness of the systems and procedures approach to office management in developing skills
    C. systems and procedures approach to office management as it relates to office costs
    D. advantages of the systems and procedures approach to office management for supervisors and office workers

9. Work guides are LEAST likely to be used when   9._____

    A. standardized forms are used
    B. a particular office task is distinct and different from all others
    C. identical tasks are to be performed in identical ways
    D. similar work methods are expected from each employee

10. According to the above passage, when an employee makes a work error, it USUALLY   10._____

    A. is quickly corrected by the supervisor
    B. necessitates a change in the work guides
    C. can be detected quickly if work guides are in use
    D. increases the probability of further errors by that employee

Questions 11-12.

DIRECTIONS: Questions 11 and 12 are to be answered SOLELY on the basis of the following passage.

The coordination of the many activities of a large public agency is absolutely essential. Coordination, as an administrative principle, must be distinguished from and is independent of cooperation. Coordination can be of either the horizontal or the vertical type. In large organizations, the objectives of vertical coordination are achieved by the transmission of orders and statements of policy down through the various levels of authority. It is an accepted generalization that the more authoritarian the organization, the more easily may vertical coordination be accomplished. Horizontal coordination is arrived at through staff work, administrative management, and conferences of administrators of equal rank. It is obvious that of the two types of coordination, the vertical kind is more important, for at best horizontal coordination only supplements the coordination effected up and down the line.

11. According to the above passage, the ease with which vertical coordination is achieved in a large agency depends upon

    11.____

    A. the extent to which control is firmly exercised from above
    B. the objectives that have been established for the agency
    C. the importance attached by employees to the orders and statements of policy transmitted through the agency
    D. the cooperation obtained at the various levels of authority

12. According to the above passage,

    12.____

    A. vertical coordination is dependent for its success upon horizontal coordination
    B. one type of coordination may work in opposition to the other
    C. similar methods may be used to achieve both types of coordination
    D. horizontal coordination is at most an addition to vertical coordination

Questions 13-17.

DIRECTIONS: Questions 13 through 17 are to be answered SOLELY on the basis of the following situation.

Assume that you are a newly appointed supervisor in the same unit in which you have been acting as a provisional for some time. You have in your unit the following workers:

WORKER I - He has always been an efficient worker. In a number of his cases, the clients have recently begun to complain that they cannot manage on the departmental budget.

WORKER II - He has been under selective supervision for some time as an experienced, competent worker. He now begins to be late for his supervisory conferences and to stress how much work he has to do.

WORKER III - He has been making considerable improvement in his ability to handle the details of his job. He now tells you, during an individual conference, that he does not need such close supervision and that he wants to operate more independently. He says that Worker II is always available when he needs a little information or help but, in general, he can manage very well by himself.

WORKER IV - He brings you a complex case for decision as to eligibility. Discussion of the case brings out the fact that he has failed to consider all the available resources adequately but has stressed the family's needs to include every extra item in the budget. This is the third case of a similar nature that this worker has brought to you recently. This worker and Worker I work in adjacent territory and are rather friendly.

In the following questions, select the option that describes the method of dealing with these workers that illustrates BEST supervisory practice.

13. With respect to supervision of Worker I, the assistant supervisor should   13.____

    A. discuss with the worker, in an individual conference, any problems that he may be having due to the increase in the cost of living
    B. plan a group conference for the unit around budgeting, as both Workers I and IV seem to be having budgetary difficulties
    C. discuss with Workers I and IV together the meaning of money as acceptance or rejection to the clients
    D. discuss with Worker I the budgetary data in each case in relation to each client's situation

14. With respect to supervision of Worker II, the supervisor should   14.____

    A. move slowly with this worker and give him time to learn that the supervisor's official appointment has not changed his attitudes or methods of supervision
    B. discuss the worker's change of attitude and ask him to analyze the reasons for his change in behavior
    C. take time to show the worker how he is avoiding his responsibility in the supervisor-worker relationship and that he is resisting supervision
    D. hold an evaluatory conference with the worker and show him how he is taking over responsibilities that are not his by providing supervision for Worker III

15. With respect to supervision of Worker III, the supervisor should discuss with this worker   15.____

    A. why he would rather have supervision from Worker II than from the supervisor
    B. the necessity for further improvement before he can go on selective supervision
    C. an analysis of the improvement that has been made and the extent to which the worker is able to handle the total job for which he is responsible
    D. the responsibility of the supervisor to see that clients receive adequate service

16. With respect to supervision of Worker IV, the supervisor should   16.____

    A. show the worker that resources figures are incomplete but that even if they were complete, the family would probably be eligible for assistance
    B. ask the worker why he is so protective of these families since there are three cases so similar
    C. discuss with the worker all three cases at the same time so that the worker may see his own role in the three situations
    D. discuss with the worker the reasons for departmental policies and procedures around budgeting

17. With respect to supervision of Workers I and IV, since these two workers are friends and would seem to be influencing each other, the supervisor should   17.____

    A. hold a joint conference with them both, pointing out how they should clear with the supervisor and not make their own rules together
    B. handle the problems of each separately in individual conferences
    C. separate them by transferring one to another territory or another unit
    D. take up the problem of workers asking help of each other rather than from the supervisor in a group meeting

Questions 18-20.

DIRECTIONS: Questions 18 through 20 are to be answered SOLELY on the basis of the following passage.

One of the key supervisory problems in a large municipal recreation department is that many leaders are assigned to isolated playgrounds or small centers, where it is difficult to observe their work regularly. Often their facilities are extremely limited. In such settings, as well as in larger recreation centers, where many recreation leaders tend to have other jobs as well, there tends to be a low level of morale and incentive. Still, it is the supervisor's task to help recreation personnel to develop pride in their work and to maintain a high level of performance. With isolated leaders, the supervisor may give advice or assistance. Leaders may be assigned to different tasks or settings during the year to maximize their productivity and provide new challenges. When it is clear that leaders are not willing to make a real effort to contribute to the department, the possibility of penalties must be considered, within the scope of departmental policy and the union contract. However, the supervisor should be constructive, encourage and assist workers to take a greater interest in their work, be innovative, and try to raise morale and to improve performance in positive ways.

18. The one of the following that would be the MOST appropriate title for the above passage is

    A. SMALL COMMUNITY CENTERS - PRO AND CON
    B. PLANNING BETTER RECREATION PROGRAMS
    C. THE SUPERVISOR'S TASK IN UPGRADING PERSONNEL PERFORMANCE
    D. THE SUPERVISOR AND THE MUNICIPAL UNION - RIGHTS AND OBLIGATIONS

18.____

19. The above passage makes clear that recreation leadership performance in ALL recreation playgrounds and centers throughout a large city is

    A. generally above average, with good morale on the part of most recreation leaders
    B. beyond description since no one has ever observed or evaluated recreation leaders
    C. a key test of the personnel department's effort to develop more effective hiring standards
    D. of mixed quality, with many recreation leaders having poor morale and a low level of achievement

19.____

20. According to the above passage, the supervisor's role is to

    A. use disciplinary action as his major tool in upgrading performance
    B. tolerate the lack of effort of individual employees since they are assigned to isolated playgrounds or small centers
    C. employ encouragement, advice, and, when appropriate, disciplinary action to improve performance
    D. inform the county supervisor whenever malfeasance or idleness is detected

20.____

Questions 21-25.

DIRECTIONS: Questions 21 through 25 are to be answered SOLELY on the basis of the following passage.

EMPLOYEE LEAVE REGULATIONS

Peter Smith, as a full-time permanent city employee under the Career and Salary Plan, earns an *annual leave allowance*. This consists of a certain number of days off a year with pay and may be used for vacation, personal business, and for observing religious holidays. As a newly appointed employee, during his first 8 years of city service, he will earn an annual leave allowance of 20 days off a year (an average of 1 2/3 days off a month). After he has finished 8 full years of working for the city, he will begin earning an additional 5 days off a year. His *annual leave allowance*, therefore, will then be 25 days a year and will remain at this amount for seven full years. He will begin earning an additional two days off a year after he has completed a total of 15 years of city employment. Therefore, in his sixteenth year of working for the city, Mr. Smith will be earning 27 days off a year as his *annual leave allowance* (an average of 2 1/4 days off a month).

A sick leave allowance of one day a month is also given to Mr. Smith, but it can be used only in cases of actual illness. When Mr. Smith returns to work after *using sick leave allowance*, he must have a doctor's note if the absence is for a total of more than 3 days, but he may also be required to show a doctor's note for absences of 1, 2, or 3 days.

21. According to the above passage, Mr. Smith's *annual leave allowance* consists of a certain number of days off a year which he
    21._____

    A. does not get paid for
    B. gets paid for at time and a half
    C. may use for personal business
    D. may not use for observing religious holidays

22. According to the above passage, after Mr. Smith has been working for the city for 9 years, his *annual leave allowance* will be _____ days a year.
    22._____

    A. 20   B. 25   C. 27   D. 37

23. According to the above passage, Mr. Smith will begin earning an average of 2 days off a month as his *annual leave allowance* after he has worked for the city for full years.
    23._____

    A. 7   B. 8   C. 15   D. 17

24. According to the above passage, Mr. Smith is given a *sick leave allowance* of
    24._____

    A. 1 day every 2 months   B. 1 day per month
    C. 1 2/3 days per month   D. 2 1/4 days a month

25. According to the above passage, when he uses *sick leave allowance*, Mr. Smith may be required to show a doctor's note
    25._____

    A. even if his absence is for only 1 day
    B. only if his absence is for more than 2 days
    C. only if his absence is for more than 3 days
    D. only if his absence is for 3 days or more

KEY (CORRECT ANSWERS)

1.	C		11.	A
2.	C		12.	D
3.	D		13.	D
4.	A		14.	A
5.	B		15.	C
6.	B		16.	C
7.	A		17.	B
8.	D		18.	C
9.	B		19.	D
10.	C		20.	C

21.	C
22.	B
23.	C
24.	B
25.	A

——————

TEST 3

Questions 1-6.

DIRECTIONS: Questions 1 through 6 are to be answered SOLELY on the basis of the following passage.

A folder is made of a sheet of heavy paper (manila, kraft, pressboard, or red rope stock)
that has been folded once so that the back is about one-half inch higher than the front. Folders are larger than the papers they contain in order to protect them. Two standard folder sizes
are *letter size* for papers that are 8 1/2" x 11" and *legal cap* for papers that are 8 1/2" x 13".

Folders are cut across the top in two ways: so that the back is straight (straight-cut) or so
that the back has a tab that projects above the top of the folder. Such tabs bear captions that
identify the contents of each folder. Tabs vary in width and position. The tabs of a set of folders that are *one-half cut* are half the width of the folder and have only two positions.

One-third cut folders have three positions, each tab occupying a third of the width of the
folder. Another standard tabbing is *one-fifth cut*, which has five positions. There are also folders with *two-fifths cut*, with the tabs in the third and fourth or fourth and fifth positions.

1. Of the following, the BEST title for the above passage is   1.____

    A.   FILING FOLDERS   B.   STANDARD FOLDER SIZES
    C.   THE USES OF THE FOLDER   D.   THE USE OF TABS

2. According to the above passage, one of the standard folder sizes is called   2.____

    A.   Kraft cut   B.   legal cap
    C.   one-half cut   D.   straight-cut

3. According to the above passage, tabs are GENERALLY placed along the _____ of the   3.____
    folder.

    A.   back   B.   front
    C.   left side   D.   right side

4. According to the above passage, a tab is GENERALLY used to   4.____

    A.   distinguish between standard folder sizes
    B.   identify the contents of a folder
    C.   increase the size of the folder
    D.   protect the papers within the folder

5. According to the above passage, a folder that is two-fifths cut has _____ tabs.   5.____

    A.   no   B.   two   C.   three   D.   five

6. According to the above passage, one reason for making folders larger than the papers   6.____
    they contain is that

    A.   only a certain size folder can be made from heavy paper
    B.   they will protect the papers
    C.   they will aid in setting up a tab system
    D.   the back of the folder must be higher than the front

Questions 7-15.

DIRECTIONS: Questions 7 through 15 are to be answered SOLELY on the basis of the follow-
               ing passage.

The City University of New York traces its origins to 1847, when the Free Academy,
which later became City College, was founded as the first tuition-free municipal college. City
and Hunter Colleges were placed under the direction of the Board of Higher Education in
1926, and Brooklyn and Queens Colleges were subsequently added to the system of municipal colleges. In 1955, Staten Island Community College, the first of the two-year colleges
sponsored by the Board of Higher Education under the program of the State University of
New York, joined the system.

In 1961, the four senior colleges and three community colleges then under the jurisdiction of the Board of Higher Education became the City University of New York, and a University Graduate Division was organized to offer programs leading to the Ph.D. Since then, the
university has undergone even more rapid growth. Today, it consists of nine senior colleges,
an upper division college which admits students at the junior level, eight community colleges,
a graduate division, and an affiliated medical center.

In the summer of 1969, the Board of Higher Education resolved that the time had come
to commit the resources of the university to meeting an urgent social need—unrestricted
access to higher education for all youths of the City. Determined to prevent the waste of
human potential represented by the thousands of high school graduates whose limited educational opportunities left them unable to meet existing admission standards, the Board
moved to adopt a policy of Open Admissions. It was their judgment that the best way of determining whether a potential student can benefit from college work is to admit him to college,
provide him with the learning assistance he needs, and then evaluate his performance.

Beginning with the class of June 1970, every New York City resident who received a high
school diploma from a public or private high school was guaranteed a place in one of the colleges of City University.

7. Of the following, the BEST title for the above passage is   7._____

    A.   A BRIEF HISTORY OF THE CITY UNIVERSITY
    B.   HIGH SCHOOLS AND THE CITY UNIVERSITY
    C.   THE COMPONENTS OF THE UNIVERSITY
    D.   TUITION-FREE COLLEGES

8. According to the above passage, which one of the following colleges of the City Univer-   8._____
    sity was ORIGINALLY called the Free Academy?

    A.   Brooklyn College   B.   City College
    C.   Hunter College   D.   Queens College

9. According to the above passage, the system of municipal colleges became the City Uni-   9._____
    versity of New York in

    A.   1926   B.   1955   C.   1961   D.   1969

10. According to the above passage, Staten Island Community College came under the juris-   10.____
    diction of the Board of Higher Education

    A. 6 years after a Graduate Division was organized
    B. 8 years before the adoption of the Open Admissions Policy
    C. 29 years after Brooklyn and Queens Colleges
    D. 29 years after City and Hunter Colleges

11. According to the above passage, the Staten Island Community College is   11.____

    A. a graduate division center
    B. a senior college
    C. a two-year college
    D. an upper division college

12. According to the above passage, the TOTAL number of colleges, divisions, and affiliated   12.____
    branches of the City University is

    A. 18   B. 19   C. 20   D. 21

13. According to the above passage, the Open Admissions Policy is designed to determine   13.____
    whether a potential student will benefit from college by PRIMARILY

    A. discouraging competition for placement in the City University among high school
       students
    B. evaluating his performance after entry into college
    C. lowering admission standards
    D. providing learning assistance before entry into college

14. According to the above passage, the FIRST class to be affected by the Open Admissions   14.____
    Policy was the

    A. high school class which graduated in January 1970
    B. City University class which graduated in June 1970
    C. high school class when graduated in June 1970
    D. City University class which graduated in June 1970

15. According to the above passage, one of the reasons that the Board of Higher Education   15.____
    initiated the policy of Open Admissions was to

    A. enable high school graduates with a background of limited educational opportuni-
       ties to enter college
    B. expand the growth of the City University so as to increase the number and variety
       of degrees offered
    C. provide a social resource to the qualified youth of the City
    D. revise admission standards to meet the needs of the City

Questions 16-18.

DIRECTIONS: Questions 16 through 18 are to be answered SOLELY on the basis of the fol-
              lowing passage.

Hereafter, all probationary students interested in transferring to community college
career programs (associate degrees) from liberal arts programs in senior colleges (bachelor

degrees) will be eligible for such transfers if they have completed no more than three semesters.

For students with averages of 1.5 or above, transfer will be automatic. Those with 1.0 to 1.5 averages can transfer provisionally and will be required to make substantial progress during the first semester in the career program. Once transfer has taken place, only those courses in which passing grades were received will be computed in the community college grade-point average.

No request for transfer will be accepted from probationary students wishing to enter the liberal arts programs at the community college.

16. According to this passage, the one of the following which is the BEST statement concerning the transfer of probationary students is that a probationary student   16._____

    A. may transfer to a career program at the end of one semester
    B. must complete three semester hours before he is eligible for transfer
    C. is not eligible to transfer to a career program
    D. is eligible to transfer to a liberal arts program

17. Which of the following is the BEST statement of academic evaluation for transfer purposes in the case of probationary students?   17._____

    A. No probationary student with an average under 1.5 may transfer.
    B. A probationary student with an average of 1.3 may not transfer.
    C. A probationary student with an average of 1.6 may transfer.
    D. A probationary student with an average of .8 may transfer on a provisional basis.

18. It is MOST likely that, of the following, the next degree sought by one who already holds the Associate in Science degree would be a(n)   18._____

    A. Assistantship in Science degree
    B. Associate in Applied Science degree
    C. Bachelor of Science degree
    D. Doctor of Philosophy degree

Questions 19-20.

DIRECTIONS: Questions 19 and 20 are to be answered SOLELY on the basis of the following passage.

Auto: Auto travel requires prior approval by the President and/or appropriate Dean and must be indicated in the *Request for Travel Authorization* form. Employees authorized to use personal autos on official College business will be reimbursed at the rate of 28¢ per mile for the first 500 miles driven and 18¢ per mile for mileage driven in excess of 500 miles. The Comptroller's Office may limit the amount of reimbursement to the expenditure that would have been made if a less expensive mode of transportation (railroad, airplane, bus, etc.) had been utilized. If this occurs, the traveler will have to pick up the excess expenditure as a personal expense.

Tolls, Parking Fees, and Parking Meter Fees are not reimbursable and may not be claimed.

19. Suppose that Professor T. gives the office assistant the following memorandum:
Used car for official trip to Albany, New York, and return. Distance from New York to
Albany is 148 miles. Tolls were $3.50 each way. Parking garage cost $3.00.
When preparing the Travel Expense Voucher for Professor T., the figure which should
be claimed for transportation is

    A. $120.88   B. $113.88   C. $82.88   D. $51.44

19.____

20. Suppose that Professor V. gives the office assistant the following memorandum:
Used car for official trip to Pittsburgh, Pennsylvania, and return.
Distance from New York to Pittsburgh is 350 miles. Tolls were $3.30, $11.40 going, and
$3.30, $2.00 returning.
When preparing the Travel Expense Voucher for Professor V., the figure which should
be claimed for transportation is

    A. $225.40   B. $176.00   C. $127.40   D. $98.00

20.____

Questions 21-25.

DIRECTIONS: Questions 21 through 25 are to be answered SOLELY on the basis of the following passage.

For a period of nearly fifteen years, beginning in the mid-1950's, higher education sus-
tained a phenomenal rate of growth. The factors principally responsible were continuing
improvement in the rate of college entrance by high school graduates, a 50 percent increase
in the size of the college-age (eighteen to twenty-one) group, and – until about 1967 – a rapid
expansion of university research activity supported by the Federal government.

Today, as one looks ahead to the year 2010, it is apparent that each of these favorable
stimuli will either be abated or turn into a negative factor. The rate of growth of the college-
age group has already diminished; and from 2000 to 2005, the size of the college-age group
has shrunk annually almost as fast as it grew from 1965 to 1970. From 2005 to 2010, this
annual decrease will slow down so that by 2010 the age group will be about the same size as
it was in 2009. This substantial net decrease in the size of the college-age group (from 1995
to 2010) will dramatically affect college enrollments since, currently, 83 percent of undergraduates are twenty-one and under, and another 11 percent are twenty-two to twenty-four.

21. Which one of the following factors is NOT mentioned in the above passage as contribut-
ing to the high rate of growth of higher education?

    A. A large increase in the size of the eighteen to twenty-one age group
    B. The equalization of educational opportunities among socio-economic groups
    C. The Federal budget impact on research and development spending in the higher
       education sector
    D. The increasing rate at which high school graduates enter college

21.____

22. Based on the information in the above passage, the size of the college-age group in
2010 will be

    A. larger than it was in 2009
    B. larger than it was in 1995
    C. smaller than it was in 2005
    D. about the same as it was in 2000

22.____

23. According to the above passage, the tremendous rate of growth of higher education started around   23.____

    A. 1950   B. 1955   C. 1960   D. 1965

24. The percentage of undergraduates who are over age 24 is MOST NEARLY   24.____

    A. 6%   B. 8%   C. 11%   D. 17%

25. Which one of the following conclusions can be substantiated by the information given in the above passage?   25.____

    A. The college-age group was about the same size in 2000 as it was in 1965.
    B. The annual decrease in the size of the college-age group from 2000 to 2005 is about the same as the annual increase from 1965 to 1970.
    C. The overall decrease in the size of the college-age group from 2000 to 2005 will be followed by an overall increase in its size from 2005 to 2010.
    D. The size of the college-age group is decreasing at a fairly constant rate from 1995 to 2010.

KEY (CORRECT ANSWERS)

1.	A		11.	C
2.	B		12.	C
3.	A		13.	B
4.	B		14.	C
5.	B		15.	A
6.	B		16.	A
7.	A		17.	C
8.	B		18.	C
9.	C		19.	C
10.	D		20.	B

21.	B
22.	C
23.	B
24.	A
25.	B

RECORD KEEPING
EXAMINATION SECTION
TEST 1

DIRECTIONS: Each question or incomplete statement is followed by several suggested answers or completions. Select the one that BEST answers the question or completes the statement. *PRINT THE LETTER OF THE CORRECT ANSWER IN THE SPACE AT THE RIGHT.*

Questions 1-7.

DIRECTIONS: In answering Questions 1 through 7, use the following master list. For each question, determine where the name would fit on the master list. Each answer choice indicates right before or after the name in the answer choice.

Aaron, Jane
Armstead, Brendan
Bailey, Charles
Dent, Ricardo
Grant, Mark
Mars, Justin
Methieu, Justine
Parker, Cathy
Sampson, Suzy
Thomas, Heather

1. Schmidt, William
   A. Right before Cathy Parker
   C. Right after Suzy Sampson
   B. Right after Heather Thomas
   D. Right before Ricardo Dent

1.____

2. Asanti, Kendall
   A. Right before Jane Aaron
   C. Right before Justine Methieu
   B. Right after Charles Bailey
   D. Right after Brendan Armstead

2.____

3. O'Brien, Daniel
   A. Right after Justine Methieu
   C. Right after Mark Grant
   B. Right before Jane Aaron
   D. Right before Suzy Sampson

3.____

4. Marrow, Alison
   A. Right before Cathy Parker
   C. Right after Mark Grant
   B. Right before Justin Mars
   D. Right after Heather Thomas

4.____

5. Grantt, Marissa
   A. Right before Mark Grant
   C. Right after Justin Mars
   B. Right after Mark Grant
   D. Right before Suzy Sampson

5.____

6. Thompson, Heath   6.____
    A. Right after Justin Mars   B. Right before Suzy Sampson
    C. Right after Heather Thomas   D. Right before Cathy Parker

DIRECTIONS: Before answering Question 7, add in all of the names from Questions 1 through 6. Then fit the name in alphabetical order based on the new list.

7. Francisco, Mildred   7.____
    A. Right before Mark Grant   B. Right after Marissa Grantt
    C. Right before Alison Marrow   D. Right after Kendall Asanti

Questions 8-10.

DIRECTIONS: In answering Questions 8 through 10, compare each pair of names and addresses. Indicate whether they are the same or different in any way.

8. William H. Pratt, J.D.   William H. Pratt, J.D.   8.____
   Attourney at Law   Attorney at Law
    A. No differences   B. 1 difference
    C. 2 differences   D. 3 differences

9. 1303 Theater Drive,; Apt. 3-B   1330 Theatre Drive,; Apt. 3-B   9.____
    A. No differences   B. 1 difference
    C. 2 differences   D. 3 differences

10. Petersdorff, Briana and Mary   Petersdorff, Briana and Mary   10.____
    A. No differences   B. 1 difference
    C. 2 differences   D. 3 differences

11. Which of the following words, if any, are misspelled?   11.____
    A. Affordable   B. Circumstansial
    C. Legalese   D. None of the above

Questions 12-13.

DIRECTIONS: Questions 12 and 13 are to be answered on the basis of the following table.

Standardized Test Results for High School Students in District #1230

	English	Math	Science	Reading
High School 1	21	22	15	18
High School 2	12	16	13	15
High School 3	16	18	21	17
High School 4	19	14	15	16

The scores for each high school in the district were averaged out and listed for each subject tested. Scores of 0-10 are significantly below College Readiness Standards. 11-15 are below College Readiness, 16-20 meet College Readiness, and 21-25 are above College Readiness.

12. If the high schools need to meet or exceed in at least half the categories   12.____
    in order to NOT be considered "at risk," which schools are considered "at risk"?
    A. High School 2   B. High School 3
    C. High School 4   D. Both A and C

13. What percentage of subjects did the district as a whole meet or exceed   13.____
    College Readiness standards?
    A. 25%   B. 50%   C. 75%   D. 100%

Questions 14-15.

DIRECTIONS: Questions 14 and 15 are to be answered on the basis of the following
information.

You have seven employees working as a part of your team: Austin, Emily, Jeremy,
Christina, Martin, Harriet, and Steve. You have just sent an e-mail informing them that
there will be a mandatory training session next week. To ensure that work still gets done,
you are offering the training twice during the week: once on Tuesday and also on
Thursday. This way half the employees will still be working while the other half attend the
training. The only other issue is that Jeremy doesn't work on Tuesdays and Harriet
doesn't work on Thursdays due to compressed work schedules.

14. Which of the following is a possible attendance roster for the first training   14.____
    session?
    A. Emily, Jeremy, Steve   B. Steve, Christina, Harriet
    C. Harriet, Jeremy, Austin   D. Steve, Martin, Jeremy

15. If Harriet, Christina, and Steve attend the training session on Tuesday, which   15.____
    of the following is a possible roster for Thursday's training session?
    A. Jeremy, Emily, and Austin   B. Emily, Martin, and Harriet
    C. Austin, Christina, and Emily   D. Jeremy, Emily, and Steve

Questions 16-20.

DIRECTIONS: In answering Questions 16 through 20, you will be given a word and will need
to choose the answer choice that is MOST similar or different to the word.

16. Which word means the SAME as *annual*?   16.____
    A. Monthly   B. Usually   C. Yearly   D. Constantly

17. Which word means the SAME as *effort*?   17.____
    A. Energy   B. Equate   C. Cherish   D. Commence

18. Which word means the OPPOSITE of *forlorn*?   18.____
    A. Neglected   B. Lethargy   C. Optimistic   D. Astonished

19. Which word means the SAME as *risk*?   19.____
    A. Admire   B. Hazard   C. Limit   D. Hesitant

20. Which word means the OPPOSITE of *translucent*?   20.____
    A. Opaque   B. Transparent   C. Luminous   D. Introverted

21. Last year, Jamie's annual salary was $50,000. Her boss called her today   21.____
    to inform her that she would receive a 20% raise for the upcoming year. How
    much more money will Jamie receive next year?
    A. $60,000   B. $10,000   C. $1,000   D. $51,000

22. You and a co-worker work for a temp hiring agency as part of their office   22.____
    staff. You both are given 6 days off per month. How many days off are you
    and your co-worker given in a year?
    A. 24   B. 72   C. 144   D. 48

23. If Margot makes $34,000 per year and she works 40 hours per week for   23.____
    all 52 weeks, what is her hourly rate?
    A. $16.34/hour   B. $17.00/hour   C. $15.54/hour D. $13.23/hour

24. How many dimes are there in $175.00?   24.____
    A. 175   B. 1,750   C. 3,500   D. 17,500

25. If Janey is three times as old as Emily, and Emily is 3, how old is Janey?   25.____
    A. 6   B. 9   C. 12   D. 15

KEY (CORRECT ANSWERS)

1.	C		11.	B
2.	D		12.	A
3.	A		13.	D
4.	B		14.	B
5.	B		15.	A
6.	C		16.	C
7.	A		17.	A
8.	B		18.	C
9.	C		19.	B
10.	A		20.	A

21.	B
22.	C
23.	A
24.	B
25.	B

TEST 2

DIRECTIONS: Each question or incomplete statement is followed by several suggested answers or completions. Select the one that BEST answers the question or completes the statement. *PRINT THE LETTER OF THE CORRECT ANSWER IN THE SPACE AT THE RIGHT.*

Questions 1-6.

DIRECTIONS: Questions 1 through 6 are to be answered on the basis of the following information.

item — name of item to be ordered
quantity — minimum number that can be ordered
beginning amount — amount in stock at start of month
amount received — amount receiving during month
ending amount — amount in stock at end of month
amount used — amount used during month
amount to order — will need at least as much of each item as used in the previous month
unit price — cost of each unit of an item
total price — total price for the order

Item	Quantity	Beginning	Received	Ending	Amount Used	Amount to Order	Unit Price	Total Price
Pens	10	22	10	8	24	20	$0.11	$2.20
Spiral notebooks	8	30	13	12			$0.25	
Binder clips	2 boxes	3 boxes	1 box	1 box			$1.79	
Sticky notes	3 packs	12 packs	4 packs	2 packs			$1.29	
Dry erase markers	1 pack (dozen)	34 markers	8 markers	40 markers			$16.49	
Ink cartridges (printer)	1 cartridge	3 cartridges	1 cartridge	2 cartridges			$79.99	
Folders	10 folders	25 folders	15 folders	10 folders			$1.08	

1. How many packs of sticky notes were used during the month?   1.____
   A. 16   B. 10   C. 12   D. 14

2. How many folders need to be ordered for next month?   2.____
   A. 15   B. 20   C. 30   D. 40

3. What is the total price of notebooks that you will need to order?   3.____
   A. $6.00   B. $0.25   C. $4.50   D. $2.75

4. Which of the following will you spend the second most money on?   4.____
   A. Ink cartridges   B. Dry erase markers
   C. Sticky notes   D. Binder clips

5. How many packs of dry erase markers should you order?   5.____
   A. 1   B. 8   C. 12   D. 0

6. What will be the total price of the file folders you order?   6.____
       A. $20.16   B. $2.16   C. $1.08   D. $4.32

Questions 7-11.

DIRECTIONS: Questions 7 through 11 are to be answered on the basis of the following table.

Number of Car Accidents, By Location and Cause, for 2014						
	Location 1		Location 2		Location 3	
Cause	Number	Percent	Number	Percent	Number	Percent
Severe Weather	10		25		30	
Excessive Speeding	20	40	5		10	
Impaired Driving	15		15	25	8	
Miscellaneous	5		15		2	4
TOTALS	50	100	60	100	50	100

7. Which of the following is the third highest cause of accidents for all three   7.____
    locations?
       A. Severe Weather   B. Impaired Driving
       C. Miscellaneous   D. Excessive Speeding

8. The average number of Severe Weather accidents per week at Location 3   8.____
    for the year (52 weeks) was MOST NEARLY
       A. 0.57   B. 30   C. 1   D. 1.25

9. Which location had the LARGEST percentage of accidents caused by   9.____
    Impaired Driving?
       A. 1   B. 2   C. 3   D. Both A and B

10. If one-third of the accidents at all three locations resulted in at least one   10.____
    fatality, what is the LEAST amount of deaths caused by accidents last year?
       A. 60   B. 106   C. 66   D. 53

11. What is the percentage of accidents caused by miscellaneous means from   11.____
    all three locations in 2014?
       A. 5%   B. 10%   C. 13%   D. 25%

12. How many pairs of the following groups of letters are exactly alike?   12.____
       ACDOBJ   ACDBOJ
       HEWBWR   HEWRWB
       DEERVS   DEERVS
       BRFQSX   BRFQSX
       WEYRVB   WEYRVB
       SPQRZA   SQRPZA

       A. 2   B. 3   C. 4   D. 5

Questions 13-19.

DIRECTIONS: Questions 13 through 19 are to be answered on the basis of the following information.

In 2012, the most current information on the American population was finished. The information was compiled by 200 volunteers in each of the 50 states. The territory of Puerto Rico, a sovereign of the United States, had 25 people assigned to compile data. In February of 2010, volunteers in each state and sovereign began collecting information. In Puerto Rico, data collection finished by January 31st, 2011, while work in the United States was completed on June 30, 2012. Each volunteer gathered data on the population of their state or sovereign. When the information was compiled, volunteers sent reports to the nation's capital, Washington, D.C. Each volunteer worked 20 hours per month and put together 10 reports per month. After the data was compiled in total, 50 people reviewed the data and worked from January 2012 to December 2012.

13. How many reports were generated from February 2010 to April 2010 in Illinois and Ohio?   13.____
     A. 3,000   B. 6,000   C. 12,000   D. 15,000

14. How many volunteers in total collected population data in January 2012?   14.____
     A. 10,000   B. 2,000   C. 225   D. 200

15. How many reports were put together in May 2012?   15.____
     A. 2,000   B. 50,000   C. 100,000   D. 100,250

16. How many hours did the Puerto Rican volunteers work in the fall (September-November)?   16.____
     A. 60   B. 500   C. 1,500   D. 0

17. How many workers were compiling or reviewing data in July 2012?   17.____
     A. 25   B. 50   C. 200   D. 250

18. What was the total amount of hours worked by Nevada volunteers in July 2010?   18.____
     A. 500   B. 4,000   C. 4,500   D. 5,000

19. How many reviewers worked in January 2013?   19.____
     A. 75   B. 50   C. 0   D. 25

20. John has to file 10 documents per shelf. How many documents would it take for John to fill 40 shelves?   20.____
     A. 40   B. 400   C. 4,500   D. 5,000

21. Jill wants to travel from New York City to Los Angeles by bike, which is approximately 2,772 miles. How many miles per day would Jill need to average if she wanted to complete the trip in 4 weeks?   21.____
     A. 100   B. 89   C. 99   D. 94

22. If there are 24 CPU's and only 7 monitors, how many more monitors do you need to have the same amount of monitors as CPU's?   22.____
    A. Not enough information   B. 17
    C. 31   D. 0

23. If Gerry works 5 days a week and 8 hours each day, and John works 3 days a week and 10 hours each day, how many more hours per year will Gerry work than John?   23.____
    A. They work the same amount of hours.
    B. 450
    C. 520
    D. 832

24. Jimmy gets transferred to a new office. The new office has 25 employees, but only 16 are there due to a blizzard. How many coworkers was Jimmy able to meet on his first day?   24.____
    A. 16   B. 25   C. 9   D. 7

25. If you do a fundraiser for charities in your area and raise $500 total, how much would you give to each charity if you were donating equal amounts to 3 of them?   25.____
    A. $250.00   B. $167.77   C. $50.00   D. $111.11

KEY (CORRECT ANSWERS)

1.	D		11.	C
2.	B		12.	B
3.	A		13.	C
4.	C		14.	A
5.	D		15.	C
6.	B		16.	C
7.	D		17.	B
8.	A		18.	B
9.	A		19.	C
10.	D		20.	B

21.	C
22.	B
23.	C
24.	A
25.	B

TEST 3

Questions 1-3.

DIRECTIONS: In answering Questions 1 through 3, choose the correctly spelled word.

1. A. allusion   B. alusion   C. allusien   D. allution   1.____

2. A. altitude   B. alltitude   C. atlitude   D. altlitude   2.____

3. A. althogh   B. allthough   C. althrough   D. although   3.____

Questions 4-9.

DIRECTIONS: In answering Questions 4 through 9, choose the answer that BEST completes the analogy.

4. Odometer is to mileage as compass is to   4.____
    A. speed   B. needle   C. hiking   D. direction

5. Marathon is to race as hibernation is to   5.____
    A. winter   B. dream   C. sleep   D. bear

6. Cup is to coffee as bowl is to   6.____
    A. dish   B. spoon   C. food   D. soup

7. Flow is to river as stagnant is to   7.____
    A. pool   B. rain   C. stream   D. canal

8. Paw is to cat as hoof is to   8.____
    A. lamb   B. horse   C. lion   D. elephant

9. Architect is to building as sculptor is to   9.____
    A. museum   B. chisel   C. stone   D. statue

Questions 10-14.

DIRECTIONS: Questions 10 through 14 are to be answered on the basis of the following graph.

Population of Carroll City Broken Down by Age and Gender (in Thousands)			
Age	Female	Male	Total
Under 15	60	60	120
15-23		22	
24-33		20	44
34-43	13	18	31
44-53	20		67
64 and Over	65	65	130
TOTAL	230	232	462

10. How many people in the city are between the ages of 15-23?   10.____
    A. 70   B. 46,000   C. 70,000   D. 225,000

11. Approximately what percentage of the total population of the city was   11.____
    female aged 24-33?
    A. 10%   B. 5%   C. 15%   D. 25%

12. If 33% of the males have a job and 55% of females don't have a job,   12.____
    which of the following statements is TRUE?
    A. Males have approximately 2,600 more jobs than females.
    B. Females have approximately 49,000 more jobs than males.
    C. Females have approximately 26,000 more jobs than males.
    D. None of the above statements are true.

13. How many females between the ages of 15-23 live in Carroll City?   13.____
    A. 67,000   B. 24,000   C. 48,000   D. 91,000

14. Assume all males 44-53 living in Carroll City are employed. If two-thirds   14.____
    of males age 44-53 work jobs outside of Carroll City, how many work within city
    limits?
    A. 31,333
    B. 15,667
    C. 47,000
    D. Cannot answer the question with the information provided

Questions 15-16.

DIRECTIONS: Questions 15 and 16 are labeled as shown. Alphabetize them for filing.
Choose the answer that correctly shows the order.

15.   (1)   AED
        (2)   OOS
        (3)   FOA
        (4)   DOM
        (5)   COB

15.____

     A. 2-5-4-3-2   B. 1-4-5-2-3   C. 1-5-4-2-3   D. 1-5-4-3-2

16.   Alphabetize the names of the people. Last names are given last.
        (1)   Lindsey Jamestown
        (2)   Jane Alberta
        (3)   Ally Jamestown
        (4)   Allison Johnston
        (5)   Lyle Moreno

16.____

     A. 2-1-3-4-5   B. 3-4-2-1-5   C. 2-3-1-4-5   D. 4-3-2-1-5

17.   Which of the following words is misspelled?

17.____

     A. disgust   B. whisper
     C. locale   D. none of the above

Questions 18-21.

DIRECTIONS: Questions 18 through 21 are to be answered on the basis of the following list of
employees.

     Robertson, Aaron
     Bacon, Gina
     Jerimiah, Trace
     Gillette, Stanley
     Jacks, Sharon

18.   Which employee name would come in third in alphabetized list?

18.____

     A. Robertson, Aaron   B. Jerimiah, Trace
     C. Gillette, Stanley   D. Jacks, Sharon

19.   Which employee's first name starts with the letter in the alphabet that is
five letters after the first letter of their last name?

19.____

     A. Jerimiah, Trace   B. Bacon, Gina
     C. Jacks, Sharon   D. Gillette, Stanley

20.   How many employees have last names that are exactly five letters long?

20.____

     A. 1   B. 2   C. 3   D. 4

21. How many of the employees have either a first or last name that starts with the letter "G"?
    A. 1   B. 2   C. 4   D. 5

21.____

Questions 22-25.

DIRECTIONS: Questions 22 through 25 are to be answered on the basis of the following chart.

Bicycle Sales (Model #34JA32)							
Country	May	June	July	August	September	October	Total
Germany	34	47	45	54	56	60	296
Britain	40	44	36	47	47	46	260
Ireland	37	32	32	32	34	33	200
Portugal	14	14	14	16	17	14	89
Italy	29	29	28	31	29	31	177
Belgium	22	24	24	26	25	23	144
Total	176	198	179	206	208	207	1166

22. What percentage of the overall total was sold to the German importer?
    A. 25.3%   B. 22%   C. 24.1%   D. 23%

22.____

23. What percentage of the overall total was sold in September?
    A. 24.1%   B. 25.6%   C. 17.9%   D. 24.6%

23.____

24. What is the average number of units per month imported into Belgium over the first four months shown?
    A. 26   B. 20   C. 24   D. 31

24.____

25. If you look at the three smallest importers, what is their total import percentage?
    A. 35.1%   B. 37.1%   C. 40%   D. 28%

25.____

KEY (CORRECT ANSWERS)

1.	A		11.	B
2.	A		12.	C
3.	D		13.	C
4.	D		14.	B
5.	C		15.	D
6.	D		16.	C
7.	A		17.	D
8.	B		18.	D
9.	D		19.	B
10.	C		20.	B

21.	B
22.	A
23.	C
24.	C
25.	A

TEST 4

DIRECTIONS: Each question or incomplete statement is followed by several suggested answers or completions. Select the one that BEST answers the question or completes the statement. *PRINT THE LETTER OF THE CORRECT ANSWER IN THE SPACE AT THE RIGHT.*

Questions 1-6.

DIRECTIONS: In answering Questions 1 through 6, choose the sentence that represents the BEST example of English grammar.

1.   A.   Joey and me want to go on a vacation next week.   1.____
     B.   Gary told Jim he would need to take some time off.
     C.   If turning six years old, Jim's uncle would teach Spanish to him.
     D.   Fax a copy of your resume to Ms. Perez and me.

2.   A.   Jerry stood in line for almost two hours.   2.____
     B.   The reaction to my engagement was less exciting than I thought it would
          be.
     C.   Carlos and me have done great work on this project.
     D.   Two parts of the speech needs to be revised before tomorrow.

3.   A.   Arriving home, the alarm was tripped.   3.____
     B.   Jonny is regarded as a stand up guy, a responsible parent, and he
          doesn't give up until a task is finished.
     C.   Each employee must submit a drug test each month.
     D.   One of the documents was incinerated in the explosion.

4.   A.   As soon as my parents get home, I told them I finished all of my chores. 4.____
     B.   I asked my teacher to send me my missing work, check my absences,
          and how did I do on my test.
     C.   Matt attempted to keep it concealed from Jenny and me.
     D.   If Mary or him cannot get work done on time, I will have to split them up.

5.   A.   Driving to work, the traffic report warned him of an accident on   5.____
          Highway 47.
     B.   Jimmy has performed well this season.
     C.   Since finishing her degree, several job offers have been given to Cam.
     D.   Our boss is creating unstable conditions for we employees.

6.   A.   The thief was described as a tall man with a wiry mustache weighing   6.____
          approximately 150 pounds.
     B.   She gave Patrick and I some more time to finish our work.
     C.   One of the books that he ordered was damaged in shipping.
     D.   While talking on the rotary phone, the car Jim was driving skidded off the
          road.

Questions 7-9.

DIRECTIONS: Questions 7 through 9 are to be answered on the basis of the following graph.

Ice Lake Frozen Flight (2002-2013)		
Year	Number of Participants	Temperature (Fahrenheit)
2002	22	4°
2003	50	33°
2004	69	18°
2005	104	22°
2006	108	24°
2007	288	33°
2008	173	9°
2009	598	39°
2010	698	26°
2011	696	30°
2012	777	28°
2013	578	32°

7.   Which two year span had the LARGEST difference between temperatures?   7.____
     A. 2002 and 2003   B. 2011 and 2012
     C. 2008 and 2009   D. 2003 and 2004

8.   How many total people participated in the years after the temperature   8.____
     reached at least 29°?
     A. 2,295   B. 1,717   C. 2,210   D. 4,543

9.   In 2007, the event saw 288 participants, while in 2008 that number   9.____
     dropped to 173. Which of the following reasons BEST explains the drop in
     participants?
     A. The event had not been going on that long and people didn't know about
         it.
     B. The lake water wasn't cold enough to have people jump in.
     C. The temperature was too cold for many people who would have normally
         participated.
     D. None of the above reasons explain the drop in participants.

10. In the following list of numbers, how many times does 4 come just after 2   10.____
     when 2 comes just after an odd number?
     23652476538986324885724863924 24
     A. 2   B. 3   C. 4   D. 5

11. Which choice below lists the letter that is as far after B as S is after N in   11.____
     the alphabet?
     A. G   B. H   C. I   D. J

Questions 12-15.

DIRECTIONS: Questions 12 through 15 are to be answered on the basis of the following directory and list of changes.

Directory		
Name	Emp. Type	Position
Julie Taylor	Warehouse	Packer
James King	Office	Administrative Assistant
John Williams	Office	Salesperson
Ray Moore	Warehouse	Maintenance
Kathleen Byrne	Warehouse	Supervisor
Amy Jones	Office	Salesperson
Paul Jonas	Office	Salesperson
Lisa Wong	Warehouse	Loader
Eugene Lee	Office	Accountant
Bruce Lavine	Office	Manager
Adam Gates	Warehouse	Packer
Will Suter	Warehouse	Packer
Gary Lorper	Office	Accountant
Jon Adams	Office	Salesperson
Susannah Harper	Office	Salesperson

Directory Updates:
- Employee e-mail address will adhere to the following guidelines: lastnamefirstname@apexindustries.com (ex. Susannah Harper is harpersusannah@apexindustries.com). Currently, employees in the warehouse share one e-mail, distribution@apexindustries.com.
- The "Loader" position was now be referred to as "Specialist I"
- Adam Gates has accepted a Supervisor position within the Warehouse and is no longer a Packer. All warehouses employees report to the two Supervisors and all office employees report to the Manager.

12. Amy Jones tried to send an e-mail to Adam Gates, but it wouldn't send. Which of the following offers the BEST explanation?
    A. Amy put Adam's first name first and then his last name.
    B. Adam doesn't check his e-mail, so he wouldn't know if he received the e-mail or not.
    C. Adam does not have his own e-mail.
    D. Office employees are not allowed to send e-mails to each other.

12.____

13. How many Packers currently work for Apex Industries?
    A. 2   B. 3   C. 4   D. 5

13.____

14. What position does Lisa Wong currently hold?
    A. Specialist I   B. Secretary
    C. Administrative Assistant   D. Loader

14.____

15. If an employee wanted to contact the office manager, which of the
    following e-mails should the e-mail be sent to?
    A. officemanager@apexindustries.com
    B. brucelavine@apexindustries.com
    C. lavinebruce@apexindustries.com
    D. distribution@apexindustries.com

15.____

Questions 16-19.

DIRECTIONS: In answering Questions 16 through 19, compare the three names, numbers or
              addresses.

16. Smiley Yarnell   Smiley Yarnel   Smily Yarnell   16.____
    A. All three are exactly alike.
    B. The first and second are exactly alike.
    C. The second and third are exactly alike.
    D. All three are different.

17. 1583 Theater Drive   1583 Theater Drive   1583 Theatre Drive   17.____
    A. All three are exactly alike.
    B. The first and second are exactly alike.
    C. The second and third are exactly alike.
    D. All three are different.

18. 3341893212   3341893212   3341893212   18.____
    A. All three are exactly alike.
    B. The first and second are exactly alike.
    C. The second and third are exactly alike.
    D. All three are different.

19. Douglass Watkins   Douglas Watkins   Douglass Watkins   19.____
    A. All three are exactly alike.
    B. The first and third are exactly alike.
    C. The second and third are exactly alike.
    D. All three are different.

Questions 20-24.

DIRECTIONS: In answering Questions 20 through 24, you will be presented with a word.
              Choose the synonym that BEST represents the word in question.

20. Flexible   20.____
    A. delicate   B. inflammable   C. strong   D. pliable

21. Alternative   21.____
    A. choice   B. moderate   C. lazy   D. value

22. Corroborate   22.____
    A. examine   B. explain   C. verify   D. explain

23. Respiration   23.____
    A. recovery   B. breathing   C. sweating   D. selfish

24. Negligent   24.____
    A. lazy   B. moderate   C. hopeless   D. lax

25. Plumber is to Wrench as Painter is to   25.____
    A. pipe   B. shop   C. hammer   D. brush

KEY (CORRECT ANSWERS)

1.	D		11.	A
2.	A		12.	C
3.	D		13.	A
4.	C		14.	A
5.	B		15.	C
6.	C		16.	D
7.	C		17.	B
8.	B		18.	A
9.	C		19.	B
10.	C		20.	D

21.	A
22.	C
23.	B
24.	D
25.	D

EXAMINATION SECTION
TEST 1

DIRECTIONS: In each of the following questions, only one of the four sentences conforms to standards of correct usage. The other three contain errors in grammar, diction, or punctuation. Select the choice in each question which BEST conforms to standards of correct usage. Consider a choice correct if it contains none of the errors mentioned above, even though there may be other ways of expressing the same thought. *PRINT THE LETTER OF THE CORRECT ANSWER IN THE SPACE AT THE RIGHT.*

1. A. Because he was ill was no excuse for his behavior.
    B. I insist that he see a lawyer before he goes to trial.
    C. He said "that he had not intended to go."
    D. He wasn't out of the office only three days.   1._____

2. A. He came to the station and pays a porter to carry his bags into the train.
    B. I should have liked to live in medieval times.
    C. My father was born in Linville. A little country town where everyone knows everyone else.
    D. The car, which is parked across the street, is disabled.   2._____

3. A. He asked the desk clerk for a clean, quiet, room.
    B. I expected James to be lonesome and that he would want to go home.
    C. I have stopped worrying because I have heard nothing further on the subject.
    D. If the board of directors controls the company, they may take actions which are disapproved by the stockholders.   3._____

4. A. Each of the players knew their place.
    B. He whom you saw on the stage is the son of an actor.
    C. Susan is the smartest of the twin sisters.
    D. Who ever thought of him winning both prizes?   4._____

5. A. An outstanding trait of early man was their reliance on omens.
    B. Because I had never been there before.
    C. Neither Mr. Jones nor Mr. Smith has completed his work.
    D. While eating my dinner, a dog came to the window.   5._____

6. A. A copy of the lease, in addition to the Rules and Regulations, are to be given to each tenant.
    B. The Rules and Regulations and a copy of the lease is being given to each tenant.
    C. A copy of the lease, in addition to the Rules and Regulations, is to be given to each tenant.
    D. A copy of the lease, in addition to the Rules and Regulations, are being given to each tenant.   6._____

7. A. Although we understood that for him music was a passion, we were disturbed by the fact that he was addicted to sing along with the soloists.
    B. Do you believe that Steven is liable to win a scholarship?
    C. Give the picture to whomever is a connoisseur of art.
    D. Whom do you believe to be the most efficient worker in the office?   7._____

8.   A.   Each adult who is sure they know all the answers will some day realize their mistake.   8.____
     B.   Even the most hardhearted villain would have to feel bad about so horrible a tragedy.
     C.   Neither being licensed teachers, both aspirants had to pass rigorous tests before being appointed.
     D.   The principal reason why he wanted to be designated was because he had never before been to a convention.

9.   A.   Being that the weather was so inclement, the party has been postponed for at least a month.   9.____
     B.   He is in New York City only three weeks and he has already seen all the thrilling sights in Manhattan and in the other four boroughs.
     C.   If you will look it up in the official directory, which can be consulted in the library during specified hours, you will discover that the chairman and director are Mr. T. Henry Long.
     D.   Working hard at college during the day and at the post office during the night, he appeared to his family to be indefatigable.

10.   A.   I would have been happy to oblige you if you only asked me to do it.   10.____
     B.   The cold weather, as well as the unceasing wind and rain, have made us decide to spend the winter in Florida.
     C.   The politician would have been more successful in winning office if he would have been less dogmatic.
     D.   These trousers are expensive; however, they will wear well.

11.   A.   All except him wore formal attire at the reception for the ambassador.   11.____
     B.   If that chair were to be blown off of the balcony, it might injure someone below.
     C.   Not a passenger, who was in the crash, survived the impact.
     D.   To borrow money off friends is the best way to lose them.

12.   A.   Approaching Manhattan on the ferry boat from Staten Island, an unforgettable sight of the skyscrapers is seen.   12.____
     B.   Did you see the exhibit of modernistic paintings as yet?
     C.   Gesticulating wildly and ranting in stentorian tones, the speaker was the sinecure of all eyes.
     D.   The airplane with crew and passengers was lost somewhere in the Pacific Ocean.

13.   A.   If one has consistently had that kind of training, it is certainly too late to change your entire method of swimming long distances.   13.____
     B.   The captain would have been more impressed if you would have been more conscientious in evacuation drills.
     C.   The passengers on the stricken ship were all ready to abandon it at the signal.
     D.   The villainous shark lashed at the lifeboat with it's tail, trying to upset the rocking boat in order to partake of it's contents.

14. A. As one whose been certified as a professional engineer, I believe that the decision   14.____
         to build a bridge over that harbor is unsound.
     B. Between you and me, this project ought to be completed long before winter arrives.
     C. He fervently hoped that the men would be back at camp and to find them busy at
         their usual chores.
     D. Much to his surprise, he discovered that the climate of Korea was like his home
         town.

15. A. An industrious executive is aided, not impeded, by having a hobby which gives him   15.____
         a fresh point of view on life and its problems.
     B. Frequent absence during the calendar year will surely mitigate against the chances
         of promotion.
     C. He was unable to go to the committee meeting because he was very ill.
     D. Mr. Brown expressed his disapproval so emphatically that his associates were
         embarassed.

16. A. At our next session, the office manager will have told you something about his   16.____
         duties and responsibilities.
     B. In general, the book is absorbing and original and have no hesitation about recom-
         mending it.
     C. The procedures followed by private industry in dealing with lateness and absence
         are different from ours.
     D. We shall treat confidentially any information about Mr. Doe, to whom we under-
         stand you have sent reports to for many years.

17. A. I talked to one official, whom I knew was fully impartial.   17.____
     B. Everyone signed the petition but him.
     C. He proved not only to be a good student but also a good athlete.
     D. All are incorrect.

18. A. Every year a large amount of tenants are admitted to housing projects.   18.____
     B. Henry Ford owned around a billion dollars in industrial equipment.
     C. He was aggravated by the child's poor behavior.
     D. All are incorrect.

19. A. Before he was committed to the asylum he suffered from the illusion that he was   19.____
         Napoleon.
     B. Besides stocks, there were also bonds in the safe.
     C. We bet the other team easily.
     D. All are incorrect.

20. A. Bring this report to your supervisor immediately.   20.____
     B. He set the chair down near the table.
     C. The capitol of New York is Albany.
     D. All are incorrect.

21. A. He was chosen to arbitrate the dispute because everyone knew he would be disin-   21.____
         terested.
     B. It is advisable to obtain the best council before making an important decision.
     C. Less college students are interested in teaching than ever before.
     D. All are incorrect.

22. A. She, hearing a signal, the source lamp flashed.   22.____
     B. While hearing a signal, the source lamp flashed.
     C. In hearing a signal, the source lamp flashed.
     D. As she heard a signal, the source lamp flashed.

23. A. Every one of the time records have been initialed in the designated spaces.   23.____
     B. All of the time records has been initialed in the designated spaces.
     C. Each one of the time records was initialed in the designated spaces.
     D. The time records all been initialed in the designated spaces.

24. A. If there is no one else to answer the phone, you will have to answer it.   24.____
     B. You will have to answer it yourself if no one else answers the phone.
     C. If no one else is not around to pick up the phone, you will have to do it.
     D. You will have to answer the phone when nobodys here to do it.

25. A. Dr. Barnes not in his office. What could I do for you?   25.____
     B. Dr. Barnes is not in his office. Is there something I can do for you?
     C. Since Dr. Barnes is not in his office, might there be something I may do for you?
     D. Is there any ways I can assist you since Dr. Barnes is not in his office?

26. A. She do not understand how the new console works.   26.____
     B. The way the new console works, she doesn't understand.
     C. She doesn't understand how the new console works.
     D. The new console works, so that she doesn't understand.

27. A. Certain changes in family income must be reported as they occur.   27.____
     B. When certain changes in family income occur, it must be reported.
     C. Certain family income changes must be reported as they occur.
     D. Certain changes in family income must be reported as they have been occuring.

28. A. Each tenant has to complete the application themselves.   28.____
     B. Each of the tenants have to complete the application by himself.
     C. Each of the tenants has to complete the application himself.
     D. Each of the tenants has to complete the application by themselves.

29. A. Yours is the only building that the construction will effect.   29.____
     B. Your's is the only building affected by the construction.
     C. The construction will only effect your building.
     D. Yours is the only building that will be affected by the construction.

30. A. There is four tests left.   30.____
     B. The number of tests left are four.
     C. There are four tests left.
     D. Four of the tests remains.

31. A. Each of the applicants takes a test.   31.____
     B. Each of the applicants take a test.
     C. Each of the applicants take tests.
     D. Each of the applicants have taken tests.

32. A. The applicant, not the examiners, are ready.   32.____
      B. The applicants, not the examiner, is ready.
      C. The applicants, not the examiner, are ready.
      D. The applicant, not the examiner, are ready.

33. A. You will not progress except you practice.   33.____
      B. You will not progress without you practicing.
      C. You will not progress unless you practice.
      D. You will not progress provided you do not practice.

34. A. Neither the director or the employees will be at the office tomorrow.   34.____
      B. Neither the director nor the employees will be at the office tomorrow.
      C. Neither the director, or the secretary nor the other employees will be at the office tomorrow.
      D. Neither the director, the secretary or the other employees will be at the office tomorrow.

35. A. In my absence he and her will have to finish the assignment.   35.____
      B. In my absence he and she will have to finish the assignment.
      C. In my absence she and him, they will have to finish the assignment.
      D. In my absence he and her both will have to finish the assignment.

KEY (CORRECT ANSWERS)

1.	B		16.	C
2.	B		17.	B
3.	C		18.	D
4.	B		19.	B
5.	C		20.	B
6.	C		21.	A
7.	D		22.	D
8.	B		23.	C
9.	D		24.	A
10.	D		25.	B
11.	A		26.	C
12.	D		27.	A
13.	C		28.	C
14.	B		29.	D
15.	A		30.	C

31. A
32. C
33. C
34. B
35. B

TEST 2

DIRECTIONS: Each question or incomplete statement is followed by several suggested answers or completions. Select the one that BEST answers the question or completes the statement. *PRINT THE LETTER OF THE CORRECT ANSWER IN THE SPACE AT THE RIGHT.*

Questions 1-4.

DIRECTIONS: Questions 1 through 4 consist of three sentences each. For each question, select the sentence which contains NO error in grammar or usage.

1. A. Be sure that everybody brings his notes to the conference.   1.____
   B. He looked like he meant to hit the boy.
   C. Mr. Jones is one of the clients who was chosen to represent the district
   D. All are incorrect.

2. A. He is taller than I.   2.____
   B. I'll have nothing to do with these kind of people.
   C. The reason why he will not buy the house is because it is too expensive.
   D. All are incorrect.

3. A. Aren't I eligible for this apartment.   3.____
   B. Have you seen him anywheres?
   C. He should of come earlier.
   D. All are incorrect.

4. A. He graduated college in 1982.   4.____
   B. He hadn't but one more line to write.
   C. Who do you think is the author of this report?
   D. All are incorrect.

Questions 5-35.

DIRECTIONS: In each of the following questions, only one of the four sentences conforms to standards of correct usage. The other three contain errors in grammar, diction, or punctuation. Select the choice in each question which BEST conforms to standards of correct usage. Consider a choice correct if it contains none of the errors mentioned above, even though there may be other ways of expressing the same thought.

5. A. It is obvious that no one wants to be a kill-joy if they can help it.   5.____
   B. It is not always possible, and perhaps it never ispossible, to judge a person's character by just looking at him.
   C. When Yogi Berra of the New York Yankees hit an immortal grandslam home run, everybody in the huge stadium including Pittsburgh fans, rose to his feet.
   D. Every one of us students must pay tuition today.

6.   A.   The physician told the young mother that if the baby is not able to digest its milk, it   6.____
should be boiled.
      B.   There is no doubt whatsoever that he felt deeply hurt because John Smith had
betrayed the trust.
      C.   Having partaken of a most delicious repast prepared by Tessie Breen, the hostess,
the horses were driven home immediately thereafter.
      D.   The attorney asked my wife and myself several questions.

7.   A.   Despite all denials, there is no doubt in my mind that   7.____
      B.   At this time everyone must deprecate the demogogic attack made by one of our
Senators on one of our most revered statesmen.
      C.   In the first game of a crucial two-game series, Ted Williams, got two singles, both of
them driving in a run.
      D.   Our visitor brought good news to John and I.

8.   A.   If he would have told me, I should have been glad to help him in his dire financial   8.____
emergency.
      B.   Newspaper men have often asserted that diplomats or so-called official spokes-
men sometimes employ equivocation in attempts to deceive.
      C.   I think someones coming to collect money for the Red Cross.
      D.   In a masterly summation, the young attorney expressed his belief that the facts
clearly militate against this opinion.

9.   A.   We have seen most all the exhibits.   9.____
      B.   Without in the least underestimating your advice, in my opinion the situation has
grown immeasurably worse in the past few days.
      C.   I wrote to the box office treasurer of the hit show that a pair of orchestra seats
would be preferable.
      D.   As the grim story of Pearl Harbor was broadcast on that fateful December 7, it was
the general opinion that war was inevitable.

10.   A.   Without a moment's hesitation, Casey Stengel said that Larry Berra works harder   10.____
than any player on the team.
      B.   There is ample evidence to indicate that many animals can run faster than any
human being.
      C.   No one saw the accident but I.
      D.   Example of courage is the heroic defense put up by the paratroopers against over-
whelming odds.

11.   A.   If you prefer these kind, Mrs. Grey, we shall be more than willing to let you have   11.____
them reasonably.
      B.   If you like these here, Mrs. Grey, we shall be more than willing to let you have them
reasonably.
      C.   If you like these, Mrs. Grey, we shall be more than willing to let you have them.
      D.   Who shall we appoint?

12.   A.   The number of errors are greater in speech than in writing.   12.____
      B.   The doctor rather than the nurse was to blame for his being neglected.
      C.   Because the demand for these books have been so great, we reduced the price.
      D.   John Galsworthy, the English novelist, could not have survived a serious illness;
had it not been for loving care.

13.   A. Our activities this year have seldom ever been as interesting as they have been this month.

       B. Our activities this month have been more interesting, or at least as interesting as those of any month this year.

       C. Our activities this month has been more interesting than those of any other month this year.

       D. Neither Jean nor her sister was at home.

13.____

14.   A. George B. Shaw's view of common morality, as well as his wit sparkling with a dash of perverse humor here and there, have led critics to term him "The Incurable Rebel."

       B. The President's program was not always received with the wholehearted endorsement of his own party, which is why the party faces difficulty in drawing up a platform for the coming election.

       C. The reason why they wanted to travel was because they had never been away from home.

       D. Facing a barrage of cameras, the visiting celebrity found it extremely difficult to express his opinions clearly.

14.____

15.   A. When we calmed down, we all agreed that our anger had been kind of unnecessary and had not helped the situation.

       B. Without him going into all the details, he made us realize the horror of the accident.

       C. Like one girl, for example, who applied for two positions.

       D. Do not think that you have to be so talented as he is in order to play in the school orchestra.

15.____

16.   A. He looked very peculiarly to me.

       B. He certainly looked at me peculiar.

       C. Due to the train's being late, we had to wait an hour.

       D. The reason for the poor attendance is that it is raining.

16.____

17.   A. About one out of four own an automobile.

       B. The collapse of the old Mitchell Bridge was caused by defective construction in the central pier.

       C. Brooks Atkinson was well acquainted with the best literature, thus helping him to become an able critic.

       D. He has to stand still until the relief man comes up, thus giving him no chance to move about and keep warm.

17.____

18.   A. He is sensitive to confusion and withdraws from people whom he feels are too noisy.

       B. Do you know whether the data is statistically correct?

       C. Neither the mayor or the aldermen are to blame.

       D. Of those who were graduated from high school, a goodly percentage went to college.

18.____

19.   A. Acting on orders, the offices were searched by a designated committee.

       B. The answer probably is nothing.

       C. I thought it to be all right to excuse them from class.

       D. I think that he is as successful a singer, if not more successful, than Mary.

19.____

20. A. $120,000 is really very little to pay for such a wellbuilt house.
    B. The creatures looked like they had come from outer space.
    C. It was her, he knew!
    D. Nobody but me knows what to do.

20._____

21. A. Mrs. Smith looked good in her new suit.
    B. New York may be compared with Chicago.
    C. I will not go to the meeting except you go with me.
    D. I agree with this editorial.

21._____

22. A. My opinions are different from his.
    B. There will be less students in class now.
    C. Helen was real glad to find her watch.
    D. It had been pushed off of her dresser.

22._____

23. A. Almost everone, who has been to California, returns with glowing reports.
    B. George Washington, John Adams, and Thomas Jefferson, were our first presidents.
    C. Mr. Walters, whom we met at the bank yesterday, is the man, who gave me my first job.
    D. One should study his lessons as carefully as he can.

23._____

24. A. We had such a good time yesterday.
    B. When the bell rang, the boys and girls went in the schoolhouse.
    C. John had the worst headache when he got up this morning.
    D. Today's assignment is somewhat longer than yesterday's.

24._____

25. A. Neither the mayor nor the city clerk are willing to talk.
    B. Neither the mayor nor the city clerk is willing to talk.
    C. Neither the mayor or the city clerk are willing to talk.
    D. Neither the mayor or the city clerk is willing to talk.

25._____

26. A. Being that he is that kind of boy, cooperation cannot be expected.
    B. He interviewed people who he thought had something to say.
    C. Stop whomever enters the building regardless of rank or office held.
    D. Passing through the countryside, the scenery pleased us.

26._____

27. A. The childrens' shoes were in their closet.
    B. The children's shoes were in their closet.
    C. The childs' shoes were in their closet.
    D. The childs' shoes were in his closet.

27._____

28. A. An agreement was reached between the defendant, the plaintiff, the plaintiff's attorney and the insurance company as to the amount of the settlement.
    B. Everybody was asked to give their versions of the accident.
    C. The consensus of opinion was that the evidence was inconclusive.
    D. The witness stated that if he was rich, he wouldn't have had to loan the money.

28._____

29. A. Before beginning the investigation, all the materials relating to the case were care- 29.____
        fully assembled.
     B. The reason for his inability to keep the appointment is because of his injury in the
        accident.
     C. This here evidence tends to support the claim of the defendant.
     D. We interviewed all the witnesses who, according to the driver, were still in town.

30. A. Each claimant was allowed the full amount of their medical expenses. 30.____
     B. Either of the three witnesses is available.
     C. Every one of the witnesses was asked to tell his story.
     D. Neither of the witnesses are right.

31. A. The commissioner, as well as his deputy and various bureau heads, were present. 31.____
     B. A new organization of employers and employees have been formed.
     C. One or the other of these men have been selected.
     D. The number of pages in the book is enough to discourage a reader.

32. A. Between you and me, I think he is the better man. 32.____
     B. He was believed to be me.
     C. Is it us that you wish to see?
     D. The winners are him and her.

33. A. Beside the statement to the police, the witness spoke to no one. 33.____
     B. He made no statement other than to the police and I.
     C. He made no statement to any one else, aside from the police.
     D. The witness spoke to no one but me.

34. A. The claimant has no one to blame but himself. 34.____
     B. The boss sent us, he and I, to deliver the packages.
     C. The lights come from mine and not his car.
     D. There was room on the stairs for him and myself.

35. A. Admission to this clinic is limited to patients' inability to pay for medical care. 35.____
     B. Patients who can pay little or nothing for medical care are treated in this clinic.
     C. The patient's ability to pay for medical care is the determining factor in his admissi-
        bility to this clinic.
     D. This clinic is for the patient's that cannot afford to pay or that can pay a little for
        medical care.

KEY (CORRECT ANSWERS)

1.	A	16.	D
2.	A	17.	B
3.	D	18.	D
4.	C	19.	B
5.	D	20.	D
6.	D	21.	A
7.	B	22.	A
8.	B	23.	D
9.	D	24.	D
10.	B	25.	B
11.	C	26.	B
12.	B	27.	B
13.	D	28.	C
14.	D	29.	D
15.	D	30.	C

31.	D
32.	A
33.	D
34.	A
35.	B

EXAMINATION SECTION
TEST 1

DIRECTIONS: Each question or incomplete statement is followed by several suggested answers or completions. Select the one that BEST answers the question or completes the statement. *PRINT THE LETTER OF THE CORRECT ANSWER IN THE SPACE AT THE RIGHT.*

Questions 1-22.

DIRECTIONS: Read through each group of words. Indicate in the space at the right the letter of the misspelled word.

1. A. miniature   B. recession   1._____
    C. accommodate   D. supress

2. A. mortgage   B. illogical   2._____
    C. fasinate   D. pronounce

3. A. calendar   B. heros   3._____
    C. ecstasy   D. librarian

4. A. initiative   B. extraordinary   4._____
    C. villian   D. exaggerate

5. A. absence   B. sense   5._____
    C. dosn't   D. height

6. A. curiosity   B. ninety   6._____
    C. truely   D. grammar

7. A. amateur   B. definate   7._____
    C. meant   D. changeable

8. A. excellent   B. studioes   8._____
    C. achievement   D. weird

9. A. goverment   B. description   9._____
    C. sergeant   D. desirable

10. A. proceed   B. anxious   10._____
    C. neice   D. precede

11. A. environment   B. omitted   11._____
    C. apparant   D. misconstrue

12. A. comparative   B. hindrance   12._____
    C. benefited   D. unamimous

13. A. embarrass   B. recommend   13._____
    C. desciple   D. argument

14. A. sophomore   B. superintendent   14._____
    C. concievable   D. disastrous

15. A. agressive   B. questionnaire   15.____
     C. occurred   D. rhythm

16. A. peaceable   B. conscientious   16.____
     C. redicule   D. deterrent

17. A. mischievious   B. writing   17.____
     C. competition   D. athletics

18. A. auxiliary   B. synonymous   18.____
     C. maneuver   D. repitition

19. A. existence   B. optomistic   19.____
     C. acquitted   D. tragedy

20. A. hypocrisy   B. parrallel   20.____
     C. exhilaration   D. prevalent

21. A. convalesence   B. infallible   21.____
     C. destitute   D. grotesque

22. A. magnanimity   B. asassination   22.____
     C. incorrigible   D. pestilence

Questions 23-40.

DIRECTIONS: In Questions 23 through 40, one sentence fragment contains an error in punctuation or capitalization. Indicate the letter of the INCORRECT sentence fragment and place it in space at the right.

23. A. Despite a year's work   23.____
     B. in a well-equipped laboratory,
     C. my Uncle failed to complete his research;
     D. now he will never graduate.

24. A. Gene, if you are going to sleep   24.____
     B. all afternoon I will enter
     C. that ladies' golf tournament
     D. sponsored by the Chamber of Commerce.

25. A. Seeing the cat slink toward the barn,   25.____
     B. the farmer's wife jumped off the
     C. ladder picked up a broom, and began
     D. shouting at the top of her voice.

26. A. Extending over southeast Idaho and   26.____
     B. northwest Wyoming, the Tetons
     C. are noted for their height; however the
     D. highest peak is actually under 14,000 feet.

27. A. "Sarah, can you recall the name
     B. of the English queen
     C. who supposedly said, 'We are not
     D. amused?'"   27.____

28. A. My aunt's graduation present to me
     B. cost, I imagine more than she could
     C. actually afford. It's a
     D. Swiss watch with numerous features.   28.____

29. A. On the left are examples of buildings
     B. from the Classical Period; two temples
     C. one of which was dedicated to Zeus; the
     D. Agora, a marketplace; and a large arch.   29.____

30. A. Tired of sonic booms, the people who
     B. live near Springfield's Municipal Airport
     C. formed an anti noise organization
     D. with the amusing name of Sound Off.   30.____

31. A. "Joe, Mrs. Sweeney said, "your family
     B. arrives Sunday. Since you'll be in
     C. the Labor Day parade, we could ask Mr.
     D. Krohn, who has a big car, to meet them."   31.____

32. A. The plumber emerged from the basement and
     B. said, "Mr. Cohen I found the trouble in
     C. your water heater. Could you move those
     D. Schwinn bikes out of my way?"   32.____

33. A. The President walked slowly to the
     B. podium, bowed to Edward Everett Hale
     C. the other speaker, and began his formal address:
     D. "Fourscore and seven years ago...."   33.____

34. A. Mr. Fontana, I hope, will arrive before
     B. the beginning of the ceremonies; however,
     C. if his plane is delayed, I have a substitute
     D. speaker who can be here at a moments' notice.   34.____

35. A. Gladys wedding dress, a satin creation,
     B. lay crumpled on the floor; her veil,
     C. torn and streaked, lay nearby. "Jilted!"
     D. shrieked Gladys. She was clearly annoyed.   35.____

36. A. Although it is poor grammar, the word
     B. hopefully has become television's newest
     C. pet expression; I hope (to use the correct
     D. form) that it will soon pass from favor.   36.____

37. A.
      B.
      C.
      D.

Plaza Apartment Hotel
103 Tower road
Hampstead, Iowa 52025
March 13, 2008

37.____

38. A. Circulation Department
      B. British History Illustrated
      C. 3000 Walnut Street
      D. Boulder Colorado 80302

38.____

39. A. Dear Sirs:
      B.   Last spring I ordered a subscription to your
      C. magazine. I had read and enjoyed the May
      D. issue containing the article titled "kings."

39.____

40. A.   I have not however, received a
      B. single issue. Will you check this?
      C. Sincerely,
      D. Maria Herrera

40.____

Questions 41-70.

DIRECTIONS: Questions 41 through 70 represent common grammatical concerns: subject-verb agreement, appropriate use of pronouns, and appropriate use of verbs. Read each sentence and indicate the letter of the grammatically CORRECT answer in the space at the right.

41. THE REIVERS, one of William Faulkner's last works, _____ made into a movie starring Steve McQueen.

    A. has been   B. have been
    C. are being   D. were

41.____

42. He _____ on the ground, his eyes fastened on an ant slowly pushing a morsel of food toward the ant hill.

    A. layed   B. laid   C. had laid   D. lay

42.____

43. Nobody in the tri-cities _____ to admit that a flood could be disastrous.

    A. are willing   B. have been willing
    C. is willing   D. were willing

43.____

44. "_____," the senator asked, "have you convinced to run against the incumbent?"

    A. Who   B. Whom   C. Whomever   D. Whomsoever

44.____

45. Of all the psychology courses that I took, Statistics 101 _____ the most demanding.

    A. was   B. are   C. is   D. were

45.____

46. Neither the conductor nor the orchestra members _____ the music to be applauded so enthusiastically.

    A. were expecting
    B. was expecting
    C. is expected
    D. has been expecting

46.____

47. The requirements for admission to the Lettermen's Club _____ posted outside the athletic director's office for months.

    A. was
    B. was being
    C. has been
    D. have been

47.____

48. Please give me a list of the people _____ to compete in the kayak race.

    A. whom you think have planned
    B. who you think has planned
    C. who you think is planning
    D. who you think are planning

48.____

49. I saw Eloise and Abelard earlier today; _____ were riding around in a fancy 1956 MG.

    A. she and him
    B. her and him
    C. she and he
    D. her and he

49.____

50. If you _____ the trunk in the attic, I'll unpack it later today.

    A. can sit
    B. are able to sit
    C. can set
    D. have sat

50.____

51. _____ all of the flour been used, or may I borrow three cups?

    A. Have
    B. Has
    C. Is
    D. Could

51.____

52. In exasperation, the cycle shop's owner suggested that _____ there too long.

    A. us boys were
    B. we boys were
    C. us boys had been
    D. we boys had been

52.____

53. Idleness as well as money _____ the root of all evil.

    A. have been
    B. were to have been
    C. is
    D. are

53.____

54. Only the string players from the quartet – Gregory, Isaac, _____ - remained after the concert to answer questions.

    A. him, and I
    B. he, and I
    C. him, and me
    D. he, and me

54.____

55. Of all the antiques that _____ for sale, Gertrude chose to buy a stupid glass thimble.

    A. was
    B. is
    C. would have
    D. were

55.____

56. The detective snapped, "Don't confuse me with theories about _____ you believe committed the crime!"

    A. who
    B. whom
    C. whomever
    D. which

56.____

57. _____ when we first called, we might have avoided our present predicament.   57.____

    A. The plumber's coming
    B. If the plumber would have come
    C. If the plumber had come
    D. If the plumber was to have come

58. We thought the sun _____ in the north until we discovered that our compass was defec-   58.____
tive.

    A. had rose   B. had risen
    C. had rised   D. had raised

59. Each play of Shakespeare's _____ more than _____ share of memorable characters.   59.____

    A. contain; its   B. contains; its
    C. contains; it's   D. contain; their

60. Our English teacher suggested to _____ seniors that either Tolstoy or Dickens _____   60.____
the outstanding novelist of the nineteenth century.

    A. we; was considered   B. we; were considered
    C. us; was considered   D. us; were considered

61. Sherlock Holmes, together with his great friend and companion Dr. Watson, _____ to   61.____
aid the woman _____ had stumbled into the room.

    A. has agreed; who   B. have agreed; whom
    C. has agreed; whom   D. have agreed; who

62. Several of the deer _____ when they spotted my backpack _____ open in the   62.____
meadow.

    A. was frightened; laying   B. were frightened; lying
    C. were frightened; laying   D. was frightened; lying

63. After the Scholarship Committee announces _____ selection, hysterics often _____.   63.____

    A. it's; occur   B. its; occur
    C. their; occur   D. their; occurs

64. I _____ the key on the table last night so you and _____ could find it.   64.____

    A. layed; her   B. lay; she
    C. laid; she   D. laid; her

65. Some of the antelope _____ wandered away from the meadow where the rancher   65.____
_____ the block of salt.

    A. has; sat   B. has; set
    C. have; had set   D. has; sets

66. Macaroni and cheese _____ best to us (that is, to Andy and _____) when Mother adds   66.____
extra cheddar cheese.

    A. tastes; I   B. tastes; me
    C. taste; me   D. taste; I

67. Frank said, "It must have been _____ called the phone company."   67.____

     A. she who   B. she whom
     C. her who   D. her whom

68. The herd _____ moving restlessly at every bolt of lightning; it was either Ted or _____   68.____
 who saw the beginning of the stampede.

     A. was; me   B. were; I
     C. was; I   D. have been; me

69. The foreman _____ his lateness by saying that his alarm clock _____ until six minutes   69.____
 before eight.

     A. explains; had not rang
     B. explained; has not rung
     C. has explained; rung
     D. explained; hadn't rung

70. Of all the coaches, Ms. Cox is the only one who _____ that Sherry dives more grace-   70.____
 fully than _____.

     A. is always saying; I
     B. is always saying; me
     C. are always saying; I
     D. were always saying; me

Questions 71-90.

DIRECTIONS: Choose the word in Questions 71 through 90 that is MOST opposite in mean-
                        ing to the italicized word.

71. *fact*   71.____

     A. statistic   B. statement
     C. incredible   D. conjecture

72. *stiff*   72.____

     A. fastidious   B. babble
     C. supple   D. apprehensive

73. *blunt*   73.____

     A. concise   B. tactful
     C. artistic   D. humble

74. *foreign*   74.____

     A. pertinent   B. comely
     C. strange   D. scrupulous

75. *anger*   75.____

     A. infer   B. pacify   C. taint   D. revile

76. *frank*   76.____

     A. earnest   B. reticent   C. post   D. expensive

77. *secure*

    A. precarious   B. acquire   C. moderate   D. frenzied

78. *petty*

    A. harmonious   B. careful   C. forthright   D. momentous

79. *concede*

    A. dispute   B. reciprocate
    C. subvert   D. propagate

80. *benefit*

    A. liquidation   B. bazaar
    C. detriment   D. profit

81. *capricious*

    A. preposterous   B. constant
    C. diabolical   D. careless

82. *boisterous*

    A. devious   B. valiant   C. girlish   D. taciturn

83. *harmony*

    A. congruence   B. discord   C. chagrin   D. melody

84. *laudable*

    A. auspicious   B. despicable
    C. acclaimed   D. doubtful

85. *adherent*

    A. partisan   B. stoic   C. renegade   D. recluse

86. *exuberant*

    A. frail   B. corpulent   C. austere   D. bigot

87. *spurn*

    A. accede   B. flail
    C. efface   D. annihilate

88. *spontaneous*

    A. hapless   B. corrosive
    C. intentional   D. willful

89. *disparage*

    A. abolish   B. exude   C. incriminate   D. extol

90. *timorous*

    A. succinct   B. chaste
    C. audacious   D. insouciant

KEY (CORRECT ANSWERS)

1.	D	21.	A	41.	A	61.	A	81.	B
2.	C	22.	B	42.	D	62.	B	82.	D
3.	B	23.	C	43.	C	63.	B	83.	B
4.	C	24.	B	44.	B	64.	C	84.	B
5.	C	25.	C	45.	A	65.	C	85.	C
6.	C	26.	C	46.	A	66.	B	86.	C
7.	B	27.	D	47.	D	67.	A	87.	A
8.	B	28.	B	48.	A	68.	C	88.	C
9.	A	29.	B	49.	C	69.	D	89.	D
10.	C	30.	C	50.	C	70.	A	90.	C
11.	C	31.	A	51.	B	71.	D		
12.	D	32.	B	52.	D	72.	C		
13.	C	33.	B	53.	C	73.	B		
14.	C	34.	D	54.	B	74.	A		
15.	A	35.	A	55.	D	75.	B		
16.	C	36.	B	56.	B	76.	B		
17.	A	37.	B	57.	C	77.	A		
18.	D	38.	D	58.	B	78.	D		
19.	B	39.	D	59.	B	79.	A		
20.	B	40.	A	60.	C	80.	C		

SPELLING
EXAMINATION SECTION
TEST 1

DIRECTIONS: In each of the following tests in this part, select the letter of the one MIS-SPELLED word in each of the following groups of words. *PRINT THE LETTER OF THE CORRECT ANSWER IN THE SPACE AT THE RIGHT.*

1. A. grateful   B. fundimental   1.____
    C. census   D. analysis

2. A. installment   B. retrieve   2.____
    C. concede   D. dissapear

3. A. accidentaly   B. dismissal   3.____
    C. conscientious   D. indelible

4. A. perceive   B. carreer   C. anticipate   D. acquire   4.____

5. A. facillity   B. reimburse   C. assortment   D. guidance   5.____

6. A. plentiful   B. across   6.____
    C. advantagous   D. similar

7. A. omission   B. pamphlet   C. guarrantee   D. repel   7.____

8. A. maintenance   B. always   8.____
    C. liable   D. anouncement

9. A. exaggerate   B. sieze   C. condemn   D. commit   9.____

10. A. pospone   B. altogether   C. grievance   D. excessive   10.____

11. A. banana   B. trafic   C. spectacle   D. boundary   11.____

12. A. commentator   B. abbreviation   12.____
    C. battaries   D. monastery

13. A. practically   B. advise   13.____
    C. pursuade   D. laboratory

14. A. fatigueing   B. invincible   14.____
    C. strenuous   D. ceiling

15. A. propeller   B. reverence   C. piecemeal   D. underneth   15.____

16. A. annonymous   B. envelope   C. transit   D. variable   16.____

17. A. petroleum   B. bigoted   C. meager   D. resistence   17.____

18. A. permissible   B. indictment   18.____
    C. fundemental   D. nowadays

19. A. thief   B. bargin   C. nuisance   D. vacant   19.____

20. A. technique   B. vengeance   C. aquatic   D. heighth   20.____

KEY (CORRECT ANSWERS)

1. B. fundamental
2. D. disappear
3. A. accidentally
4. B. career
5. A. facility

6. C. advantageous
7. C. guarantee
8. D. announcement
9. B. seize
10. A. postpone

11. B. traffic
12. C. batteries
13. C. persuade
14. A. fatiguing
15. D. underneath

16. A. anonymous
17. D. resistance
18. C. fundamental
19. B. bargain
20. D. height

———

TEST 2

DIRECTIONS: In each of the following tests in this part, select the letter of the one MIS-SPELLED word in each of the following groups of words. *PRINT THE LETTER OF THE CORRECT ANSWER IN THE SPACE AT THE RIGHT.*

1. A. apparent   B. superintendent   1.____
    C. releive   D. calendar

2. A. foreign   B. negotiate   C. typical   D. disipline   2.____

3. A. posponed   B. argument   3.____
    C. susceptible   D. deficit

4. A. preferred   B. column   C. peculiar   D. equiped   4.____

5. A. exaggerate   B. disatisfied   5.____
    C. repetition   D. already

6. A. livelihood   B. physician   C. obsticle   D. strategy   6.____

7. A. courageous   B. ommission   C. ridiculous   D. awkward   7.____

8. A. sincerely   B. abundance   C. negligable   D. elementary   8.____

9. A. obsolete   B. mischievous   9.____
    C. enumerate   D. atheletic

10. A. fiscel   B. beneficiary   10.____
    C. concede   D. translate

11. A. segregate   B. excessivly   C. territory   D. obstacle   11.____

12. A. unnecessary   B. monopolys   12.____
    C. harmonious   D. privilege

13. A. sinthetic   B. intellectual   13.____
    C. gracious   D. archaic

14. A. beneficial   B. fulfill   C. sarcastic   D. disolve   14.____

15. A. umbrella   B. sentimental   15.____
    C. inefficent   D. psychiatrist

16. A. noticable   B. knapsack   C. librarian   D. meant   16.____

17. A. conference   B. upheaval   C. vulger   D. odor   17.____

18. A. surmount   B. pentagon   C. calorie   D. inumerable   18.____

19. A. classifiable   B. moisturize   19.____
    C. monitor   D. assesment

20. A. thermastat   B. corrupting   C. approach   D. thinness   20.____

147

KEY (CORRECT ANSWERS)

1. C. relieve
2. D. discipline
3. A. postponed
4. D. equipped
5. B. dissatisfied

6. C. obstacle
7. B. omission
8. C. negligible
9. D. athletic
10. A. fiscal

11. B. excessively
12. B. monopolies
13. A. synthetic
14. D. dissolve
15. C. inefficient

16. A. noticeable
17. C. vulgar
18. D. innumerable
19. D. assessment
20. A. thermostat

TEST 3

DIRECTIONS: In each of the following tests in this part, select the letter of the one MIS-
SPELLED word in each of the following groups of words. *PRINT THE LETTER
OF THE CORRECT ANSWER IN THE SPACE AT THE RIGHT.*

1.	A.	typical	B.	descend	C.	summarize	D.	continuel	1.____
2.	A.	courageous	B.	recomend	C.	omission	D.	eliminate	2.____
3.	A. C.	compliment auxilary			B. D.	illuminate installation			3.____
4.	A. C.	preliminary syllable			B. D.	aquainted analysis			4.____
5.	A.	accustomed	B.	negligible	C.	interupted	D.	bulletin	5.____
6.	A.	summoned	B.	managment	C.	mechanism	D.	sequence	6.____
7.	A.	commitee	B.	surprise	C.	noticeable	D.	emphasize	7.____
8.	A.	occurrance	B.	likely	C.	accumulate	D.	grievance	8.____
9.	A. C.	obstacle baggage			B. D.	particuliar fascinating			9.____
10.	A. C.	innumerable applicant			B. D.	seize dictionery			10.____
11.	A.	monkeys	B.	rigid	C.	unnatural	D.	roomate	11.____
12.	A.	surveying	B.	figurative	C.	famous	D.	curiosety	12.____
13.	A. C.	rodeo calendar			B. D.	inconcievable magnificence			13.____
14.	A.	handicaped	B.	glacier	C.	defiance	D.	emperor	14.____
15.	A.	schedule	B.	scrawl	C.	seclusion	D.	sissors	15.____
16.	A.	tissues	B.	tomatos	C.	tyrants	D.	tragedies	16.____
17.	A.	casette	B.	graceful	C.	penicillin	D.	probably	17.____
18.	A.	gnawed	B.	microphone	C.	clinicle	D.	batch	18.____
19.	A.	amateur	B.	altitude	C.	laborer	D.	expence	19.____
20.	A.	mandate	B.	flexable	C.	despise	D.	verify	20.____

KEY (CORRECT ANSWERS)

1. D. continual
2. B. recommend
3. C. auxiliary
4. B. acquainted
5. C. interrupted

6. B. management
7. A. committee
8. A. occurrence
9. B. particular
10. D. dictionary

11. D. roommate
12. D. curiosity
13. B. inconceivable
14. A. handicapped
15. D. scissors

16. B. tomatoes
17. A. cassette
18. C. clinical
19. D. expense
20. B. flexible

TEST 4

DIRECTIONS: In each of the following tests in this part, select the letter of the one MIS-
SPELLED word in each of the following groups of words. *PRINT THE LETTER
OF THE CORRECT ANSWER IN THE SPACE AT THE RIGHT.*

1.   A.   primery   B.   mechanic   C.   referred   D.   admissible   1._____

2.   A.   cessation   B.   beleif   C.   aggressive   D.   allowance   2._____

3.   A.   leisure   B.   authentic   3._____
     C.   familiar   D.   contemptable

4.   A.   volume   B.   forty   C.   dilemma   D.   seldum   4._____

5.   A.   discrepancy   B.   aquisition   5._____
     C.   exorbitant   D.   lenient

6.   A.   simultanous   B.   penetrate   6._____
     C.   revision   D.   conspicuous

7.   A.   ilegible   B.   gracious   C.   profitable   D.   obedience   7._____

8.   A.   manufacturer   B.   authorize   8._____
     C.   compelling   D.   pecular

9.   A.   anxious   B.   rehearsal   C.   handicaped   D.   tendency   9._____

10. A.   meticulous   B.   accompaning   10._____
     C.   initiative   D.   shelves

11. A.   hammaring   B.   insecticide   11._____
     C.   capacity   D.   illogical

12. A.   budget   B.   luminous   C.   aviation   D.   lunchon   12._____

13. A.   moniter   B.   bachelor   13._____
     C.   pleasurable   D.   omitted

14. A.   monstrous   B.   transistor   C.   narrative   D.   anziety   14._____

15. A.   engagement   B.   judical   C.   pasteurize   D.   tried   15._____

16. A.   fundimental   B.   innovation   16._____
     C.   perpendicular   D.   extravagant

17. A.   bookkeeper   B.   brutality   C.   gymnaseum   D.   cemetery   17._____

18. A.   sturdily   B.   pretentious   18._____
     C.   gourmet   D.   enterance

19. A.   resturant   B.   tyranny   19._____
     C.   kindergarten   D.   ancestry

20. A.   benefit   B.   possess   C.   speciman   D.   noticing   20._____

KEY (CORRECT ANSWERS)

1. A. primary
2. B. belief
3. D. contemptible
4. D. seldom
5. B. acquisition

6. A. simultaneous
7. A. illegible
8. D. peculiar
9. C. handicapped
10. B. accompanying

11. A. hammering
12. D. luncheon
13. A. monitor
14. D. anxiety
15. B. judicial

16. A. fundamental
17. C. gymnasium
18. D. entrance
19. A. restaurant
20. C. specimen

_____

TEST 5

DIRECTIONS: In each of the following tests in this part, select the letter of the one MIS-SPELLED word in each of the following groups of words. *PRINT THE LETTER OF THE CORRECT ANSWER IN THE SPACE AT THE RIGHT.*

1. A. arguing   B. correspondance   1._____
    C. forfeit   D. dissension

2. A. occasion   B. description   2._____
    C. prejudice   D. elegible

3. A. accomodate   B. initiative   C. changeable   D. enroll   3._____

4. A. temporary   B. insistent   C. benificial   D. separate   4._____

5. A. achieve   B. dissappoint   5._____
    C. unanimous   D. judgment

6. A. procede   B. publicly   C. sincerity   D. successful   6._____

7. A. deceive   B. goverment   C. preferable   D. repetitive   7._____

8. A. emphasis   B. skillful   C. advisible   D. optimistic   8._____

9. A. tendency   B. rescind   C. crucial   D. noticable   9._____

10. A. privelege   B. abbreviate   C. simplify   D. divisible   10._____

11. A. irresistible   B. varius   11._____
    C. mutual   D. refrigerator

12. A. amateur   B. distinguish   12._____
    C. rehearsal   D. poision

13. A. biased   B. ommission   C. precious   D. coordinate   13._____

14. A. calculated   B. enthusiasm   C. sincerely   D. parashute   14._____

15. A. sentry   B. materials   C. incredable   D. budget   15._____

16. A. chocolate   B. instrument   C. volcanoe   D. shoulder   16._____

17. A. ancestry   B. obscure   C. intention   D. ninty   17._____

18. A. artical   B. bracelet   C. beggar   D. hopeful   18._____

19. A. tournament   B. sponsor   19._____
    C. perpendiclar   D. dissolve

20. A. yeild   B. physician   C. greasiest   D. admitting   20._____

KEY (CORRECT ANSWERS)

1. B. correspondence
2. D. eligible
3. A. accommodate
4. C. beneficial
5. B. disappoint

6. A. proceed
7. B. government
8. C. advisable
9. D. noticeable
10. A. privilege

11. B. various
12. D. poison
13. B. omission
14. D. parachute
15. C. incredible

16. C. volcano
17. D. ninety
18. A. article
19. C. perpendicular
20. A. yield

TEST 6

DIRECTIONS: In each of the following tests in this part, select the letter of the one MIS-
SPELLED word in each of the following groups of words. *PRINT THE LETTER
OF THE CORRECT ANSWER IN THE SPACE AT THE RIGHT.*

1.   A. achievment   B. maintenance   1._____
     C. questionnaire   D. all are correct

2.   A. prevelant   B. pronunciation   2._____
     C. separate   D. all are correct

3.   A. permissible   B. relevant   3._____
     C. seize   D. all are correct

4.   A. corroborate   B. desparate   4._____
     C. eighth   D. all are correct

5.   A. exceed   B. feasibility   5._____
     C. psycological   D. all are correct

6.   A. parallel   B. aluminum   C. calendar   D. eigty   6._____

7.   A. microbe   B. ancient   C. autograph   D. existance   7._____

8.   A. plentiful   B. skillful   C. amoung   D. capsule   8._____

9.   A. erupt   B. quanity   C. opinion   D. competent   9._____

10. A. excitement   B. discipline C. luncheon   D. regreting   10._____

11. A. magazine   B. expository C. imitation   D. permenent   11._____

12. A. ferosious   B. machinery   12._____
     C. precise   D. magnificent

13. A. conceive   B. narritive   C. separation   D. management   13._____

14. A. muscular   B. witholding C. pickle   D. glacier   14._____

15. A. vehicel   B. mismanage   15._____
     C. correspondence   D. dissatisfy

16. A. sentince   B. bulletin   C. notice   D. definition   16._____

17. A. appointment   B. exactly   17._____
     C. typest   D. light

18. A. penalty   B. suparvise   C. consider   D. division   18._____

19. A. schedule   B. accurate   C. corect   D. simple   19._____

20. A. suggestion   B. installed   C. proper   D. agincy   20._____

KEY (CORRECT ANSWERS)

1. A. achievement
2. A. prevalent
3. D all are correct
4. B. desperate
5. C. psychological

6. D. eighty
7. D. existence
8. C. among
9. B. quantity
10. D. regretting

11. D. permanent
12. A. ferocious
13. B. narrative
14. B. withholding
15. A. vehicle

16. A. sentence
17. C. typist
18. B. supervise
19. C. correct
20. D. agency

TEST 7

DIRECTIONS: In each of the following tests in this part, select the letter of the one MIS-SPELLED word in each of the following groups of words. *PRINT THE LETTER OF THE CORRECT ANSWER IN THE SPACE AT THE RIGHT.*

1.	A.	symtom	B.	serum	C.	antiseptic	D.	aromatic	1._____
2.	A.	register	B.	registrar	C.	purser	D.	burser	2._____
3.	A.	athletic	B.	tragedy	C.	batallion	D.	sophomore	3._____
4.	A.	latent	B.	godess	C.	aisle	D.	whose	4._____
5.	A.	rhyme	B.	rhythm	C.	thime	D.	thine	5._____
6.	A.	eighth	B.	exaggerate	C.	electorial	D.	villain	6._____

7.   A. statute   B. superintendent   7._____
       C. iresistible   D. colleague

8.	A.	sieze	B.	therefor	C.	auxiliary	D.	changeable	8._____
9.	A.	siege	B.	knowledge	C.	lieutenent	D.	weird	9._____
10.	A.	acquitted	B.	polititian	C.	professor	D.	conqueror	10._____
11.	A.	changeable	B.	chargeable	C.	salable	D.	useable	11._____
12.	A.	promissory	B.	prisoner	C.	excellent	D.	tyrrany	12._____

13.   A. conspicuous   B. essance   13._____
       C. comparative   D. brilliant

14.	A.	notefying	B.	accentuate	C.	adhesive	D.	primarily	14._____
15.	A.	exercise	B.	sublime	C.	stuborn	D.	shameful	15._____
16.	A.	presume	B.	transcript	C.	strech	D.	wizard	16._____

17.   A. specify   B. regional   17._____
       C. arbitrary   D. segragation

18.   A. requirement   B. happiness   18._____
       C. achievement   D. gentlely

19.	A.	endurance	B.	fusion	C.	balloon	D.	enormus	19._____
20.	A.	luckily	B.	schedule	C.	simplicity	D.	sanwich	20._____

KEY (CORRECT ANSWERS)

1. A. symptom
2. D. bursar
3. C. battalion
4. B. goddess
5. C. thyme

6. C. electoral
7. C. irresistible
8. A. seize
9. C. lieutenant
10. B. politician

11. D. usable
12. D. tyranny
13. B. essence
14. A. notifying
15. C. stubborn

16. C. stretch
17. D. segregation
18. D. gently
19. D. enormous
20. D. sandwich

———

TEST 8

DIRECTIONS: In each of the following tests in this part, select the letter of the one MIS-SPELLED word in each of the following groups of words. *PRINT THE LETTER OF THE CORRECT ANSWER IN THE SPACE AT THE RIGHT.*

| 1. | A. maintain | | B. maintainance | | 1.____ |
| | C. sustain | | D. sustenance | | |

| 2. | A. portend | | B. portentious | | 2.____ |
| | C. pretend | | D. pretentious | | |

| 3. | A. prophesize | | B. prophesies | | 3.____ |
| | C. farinaceous | | D. spaceous | | |

| 4. | A. choose | B. chose | C. choosen | D. chasten | 4.____ |

| 5. | A. censure | | B. censorious | | 5.____ |
| | C. pleasure | | D. pleasurible | | |

| 6. | A. cover | B. coverage | C. adder | D. adege | 6.____ |

| 7. | A. balloon | B. diregible | C. direct | D. descent | 7.____ |

| 8. | A. whemsy | B. crazy | C. flimsy | D. lazy | 8.____ |

| 9. | A. derision | B. pretention | C. sustention | D. contention | 9.____ |

| 10. | A. question | | B. questionaire | | 10.____ |
| | C. legion | | D. legionary | | |

| 11. | A. chattle | B. cattle | C. dismantle | D. kindle | 11.____ |

| 12. | A. canal | B. cannel | C. chanel | D. colonel | 12.____ |

| 13. | A. hemorrage | B. storage | C. manage | D. foliage | 13.____ |

| 14. | A. surgeon | B. sturgeon | C. luncheon | D. stancheon | 14.____ |

| 15. | A. diploma | B. commission | C. dependent | D. luminious | 15.____ |

| 16. | A. likelihood | B. blizzard | C. machanical | D. suppress | 16.____ |

| 17. | A. commercial | B. releif | C. disposal | D. endeavor | 17.____ |

| 18. | A. operate | B. bronco | C. excaping | D. grammar | 18.____ |

| 19. | A. orchard | B. collar | C. embarass | D. distant | 19.____ |

| 20. | A. sincerly | B. possessive | C. weighed | D. waist | 20.____ |

KEY (CORRECT ANSWERS)

1. B. maintenance
2. B. portentous
3. D. spacious
4. C. chosen
5. D. pleasurable

6. D. adage
7. B. dirigible
8. A. whimsy
9. B. pretension
10. B. questionnaire

11. A. chattel
12. C. channel
13. A. hemorrhage
14. D. stanchion
15. D. luminous

16. C. mechanical
17. B. relief
18. C. escaping
19. C. embarrass
20. A. sincerely

TEST 9

DIRECTIONS: In each of the following tests in this part, select the letter of the one MIS-SPELLED word in each of the following groups of words. *PRINT THE LETTER OF THE CORRECT ANSWER IN THE SPACE AT THE RIGHT.*

1. A. statute   B. stationary   1._____
    C. staturesque   D. stature

2. A. practicible   B. practical   2._____
    C. particle   D. reticule

3. A. plague   B. plaque   C. ague   D. aigrete   3._____

4. A. theology   B. idealogy   C. psychology   D. philology   4._____

5. A. dilema   B. stamina   C. feminine   D. strychnine   5._____

6. A. deceit   B. benefit   C. grieve   D. hienous   6._____

7. A. commensurable   B. measurable   7._____
    C. duteable   D. salable

8. A. homogeneous   B. heterogeneous   8._____
    C. advantageous   D. religeous

9. A. criticize   B. dramatise   C. exorcise   D. exercise   9._____

10. A. ridiculous   B. comparable   C. merciful   D. cotten   10._____

11. A. antebiotic   B. stitches   C. pitiful   D. sneaky   11._____

12. A. amendment   B. candadate   12._____
    C. accountable   D. recommendation

13. A. avocado   B. recruit   C. tripping   D. probally   13._____

14. A. calendar   B. desirable   C. familar   D. vacuum   14._____

15. A. deteriorate   B. elligible   15._____
    C. liable   D. missile

16. A. amateur   B. competent   16._____
    C. mischeivous   D. occasion

17. A. friendliness   B. saleries   17._____
    C. cruelty   D. ammunition

18. A. wholesome   B. cieling   C. stupidity   D. eligible   18._____

19. A. comptroller   B. traveled   19._____
    C. accede   D. procede

20. A. Britain   B. Brittainica   20._____
    C. conductor   D. vendor

KEY (CORRECT ANSWERS)

1. C. statuesque
2. A. practicable
3. D. aigrette
4. B. ideology
5. A. dilemma

6. D. heinous
7. C. dutiable
8. D. religious
9. B. dramatize
10. D. cotton

11. A. antibiotic
12. B. candidate
13. D. probably
14. C. familiar
15. B. eligible

16. C. mischievous
17. B. salaries
18. B. ceiling
19. D. proceed
20. B. Brittanica

TEST 10

DIRECTIONS: In each of the following tests in this part, select the letter of the one MIS-
SPELLED word in each of the following groups of words. *PRINT THE LETTER
OF THE CORRECT ANSWER IN THE SPACE AT THE RIGHT.*

1. A. lengthen   B. region   C. gases   D. inspecter   1.____

2. A. imediately   B. forbidden   2.____
    C. complimentary   D. aeronautics

3. A. continuous   B. paralel   C. opposite   D. definite   3.____

4. A. Antarctic   B. Wednesday   C. Febuary   D. Hungary   4.____

5. A. transmission   B. exposure   5.____
    C. pistol   D. customery

6. A. juvinile   B. martyr   6.____
    C. deceive   D. collaborate

7. A. unnecessary   B. repetitive   7.____
    C. cancellation   D. airey

8. A. transit   B. availible   C. objection   D. galaxy   8.____

9. A. ineffective   B. believeable   9.____
    C. arrangement   D. aggravate

10. A. possession   B. progress   C. reception   D. predjudice   10.____

11. A. congradulate   B. percolate   11.____
    C. major   D. leisure

12. A. convenience   B. privilige   12.____
    C. emerge   D. immerse

13. A. erasable   B. inflammable   13.____
    C. audable   D. laudable

14. A. final   B. fines   C. finis   D. Finish   14.____

15. A. emitted   B. representative   15.____
    C. discipline   D. insistance

16. A. diphthong   B. rarified   C. library   D. recommend   16.____

17. A. compel   B. belligerent   17.____
    C. successful   D. sargeant

18. A. dispatch   B. dispise   C. dispose   D. dispute   18.____

19. A. administrator   B. adviser   19.____
    C. diner   D. celluler

20. A. ignite   B. ignision   C. igneous   D. ignited   20.____

KEY (CORRECT ANSWERS)

1. D. inspector
2. A. immediately
3. B. parallel
4. C. February
5. D. customary

6. A. juvenile
7. D. airy
8. B. available
9. B. believable
10. D. prejudice

11. A. congratulate
12. B. privilege
13. C. audible
14. D. Finnish
15. D. insistence

16. B. rarefied
17. D. sergeant
18. B. despise
19. D. cellular
20. B. ignition

———

TEST 11

DIRECTIONS: In each of the following tests in this part, select the letter of the one MIS-
SPELLED word in each of the following groups of words. *PRINT THE LETTER
OF THE CORRECT ANSWER IN THE SPACE AT THE RIGHT.*

1. A. repellent   B. secession   C. sebaceous   D. saxaphone   1. ____

2. A. navel   B. counteresolution   2. ____
    C. marginalia   D. perceptible

3. A. Hammerskjold   B. Nehru   3. ____
    C. U Thamt   D. Khrushchev

4. A. perculate   B. periwinkle   4. ____
    C. perigee   D. retrogression

5. A. buccaneer   B. tobacco   C. buffalo   D. oscilate   5. ____

6. A. siege   B. wierd   C. seize   D. cemetery   6. ____

7. A. equaled   B. bigoted   7. ____
    C. benefited   D. kaleideoscope

8. A. blamable   B. bullrush   8. ____
    C. questionnaire   D. irascible

9. A. tobagganed   B. acquiline   9. ____
    C. capillary   D. cretonne

10. A. daguerrotype   B. elegiacal   10. ____
    C. iridescent   D. inchoate

11. A. bayonet   B. braggadocio   11. ____
    C. corollary   D. connoiseur

12. A. equinoctial   B. fusillade   12. ____
    C. fricassee   D. potpouri

13. A. octameter   B. impressario   13. ____
    C. hyetology   D. hieroglyphics

14. A. innanity   B. idyllic   C. fylfot   D. inimical   14. ____

15. A. liquefy   B. rarefy   C. putrify   D. sapphire   15. ____

16. A. canonical   B. stupified   16. ____
    C. millennium   D. memorabilia

17. A. paraphenalia   B. odyssey   17. ____
    C. onomatopoeia   D. osseous

18. A. peregrinate   B. pecadillo   18. ____
    C. reptilian   D. uxorious

19. A. pharisaical   B. vicissitude   19. ____
    C. puissance   D. wainright

20. A. holocaust   B. tesselate   C. scintilla   D. staccato   20. ____

KEY (CORRECT ANSWERS)

1. D. saxophone
2. B. counterresolution
3. C. U Thant
4. A. percolate
5. D. oscillate

6. B. weird
7. D. kaleidoscope
8. B. bulrush
9. B. aquiline
10. A. daguerreotype

11. D. connoisseur
12. D. potpourri
13. B. impresario
14. A. inanity
15. C. putrefy

16. B. stupefied
17. A. paraphernalia
18. B. peccadillo
19. D. wainwright
20. B. tessellate

———

TEST 12

DIRECTIONS: In each of the following tests in this part, select the letter of the one MIS-SPELLED word in each of the following groups of words. *PRINT THE LETTER OF THE CORRECT ANSWER IN THE SPACE AT THE RIGHT.*

1. A. questionnaire   B. gondoleer   C. chandelier   D. acquiescence   1._____

2. A. surveillance   B. surfeit   C. vaccinate   D. belligerent   2._____

3. A. occassionally   B. recurrence   C. silhouette   D. incessant   3._____

4. A. transferral   B. benefical   C. descendant   D. dependent   4._____

5. A. separately   B. flouresence C. deterrent   D. parallel   5._____

6. A. acquittal   B. enforceable C. counterfeit   D. indispensible   6._____

7. A. susceptible   B. accelarate   C. exhilarate   D. accommodation   7._____

8. A. impedimenta   B. collateral   C. liason   D. epistolary   8._____

9. A. inveigle   B. panegyric   C. reservoir   D. manuver   9._____

10. A. synopsis   B. paraphernalia C. affidavit   D. subpoena   10._____

11. A. grosgrain   B. vermilion   C. abbatoir   D. connoiseur   11._____

12. A. gabardine   B. camoflage   C. hemorrhage   D. contraband   12._____

13. A. opprobrious   B. defalcate   13._____
    C. fiduciery   D. recommendations

14. A. nebulous   B. necessitate C. impricate   D. discrepancy   14._____

15. A. discrete   B. condesension C. condign   D. condiment   15._____

16. A. cavalier   B. effigy   C. legitimatly   D. misalliance   16._____

17. A. rheumatism   B. vaporous   C. cannister   D. hallucinations   17._____

18. A. paleonthology   B. octogenarian C. gradient   D. impingement   18._____

19. A. fusilade   B. fusilage   C. ensilage   D. desiccate   19._____

20. A. rationale   B. raspberry   C. reprobate   D. varigated   20._____

KEY (CORRECT ANSWERS)

1. B. gondolier
2. A. surveillance
3. A. occasionally
4. B. beneficial
5. B. fluorescence

6. D. indispensable
7. B. accelerate
8. C. liaison
9. D. maneuver
10. B. paraphernalia

11. D. connoisseur
12. B. camouflage
13. C. fiduciary
14. C. imprecate
15. B. condescension

16. C. legitimately
17. C. canister
18. A. paleontology
19. A. fusillade
20. D. variegated

PREPARING WRITTEN MATERIAL

PARAGRAPH REARRANGEMENT
COMMENTARY

The sentences which follow are in scrambled order. You are to rearrange them in proper order and indicate the letter choice containing the correct answer at the space at the right.

Each group of sentences in this section is actually a paragraph presented in scrambled order. Each sentence in the group has a place in that paragraph; no sentence is to be left out. You are to read each group of sentences and decide upon the best order in which to put the sentences so as to form as well-organized paragraph.

The questions in this section measure the ability to solve a problem when all the facts relevant to its solution are not given.

More specifically, certain positions of responsibility and authority require the employee to discover connections between events sometimes, apparently, unrelated. In order to do this, the employee will find it necessary to correctly infer that unspecified events have probably occurred or are likely to occur. This ability becomes especially important when action must be taken on incomplete information.

Accordingly, these questions require competitors to choose among several suggested alternatives, each of which presents a different sequential arrangement of the events. Competitors must choose the MOST logical of the suggested sequences.

In order to do so, they may be required to draw on general knowledge to infer missing concepts or events that are essential to sequencing the given events. Competitors should be careful to infer only what is essential to the sequence. The plausibility of the wrong alternatives will always require the inclusion of unlikely events or of additional chains of events which are NOT essential to sequencing the given events.

It's very important to remember that you are looking for the best of the four possible choices, and that the best choice of all may not even be one of the answers you're given to choose from.

There is no one right way to solve these problems. Many people have found it helpful to first write out the order of the sentences, as they would have arranged them, on their scrap paper before looking at the possible answers. If their optimum answer is there, this can save them some time. If it isn't, this method can still give insight into solving the problem. Others find it most helpful to just go through each of the possible choices, contrasting each as they go along. You should use whatever method feels comfortable, and works, for you.

While most of these types of questions are not that difficult, we've added a higher percentage of the difficult type, just to give you more practice. Usually there are only one or two questions on this section that contain such subtle distinctions that you're unable to answer confidently, and you then may find yourself stuck deciding between two possible choices, neither of which you're sure about.

EXAMINATION SECTION
TEST 1

DIRECTIONS: The sentences that follow are in scrambled order. You are to rearrange them in proper order and indicate the letter choice containing the correct answer. *PRINT THE LETTER OF THE CORRECT ANSWER IN THE SPACE AT THE RIGHT.*

1. Below are four statements labeled W., X., Y., and Z.   1.____
    - W.   He was a strict and fanatic drillmaster.
    - X.   The word is always used in a derogatory sense and generally shows resentment and anger on the part of the user.
    - Y.   It is from the name of this Frenchman that we derive our English word, martinet.
    - Z.   Jean Martinet was the Inspector-General of Infantry during the reign of King Louis XIV.

    The *PROPER* order in which these sentences should be placed in a paragraph is:

    A. X, Z, W, Y   B. X, Z, Y, W   C. Z, W, Y, X   D. Z, Y, W, X

2. In the following paragraph, the sentences which are numbered, have been jumbled.   2.____
    1. Since then it has undergone changes.
    2. It was incorporated in 1955 under the laws of the State of New York.
    3. Its primary purpose, a cleaner city, has, however, remained the same.
    4. The Citizens Committee works in cooperation with the Mayor's Inter-departmental Committee for a Clean City.

    The order in which these sentences should be arranged to form a well-organized paragraph is:

    A. 2, 4, 1, 3   B. 3, 4, 1, 2   C. 4, 2, 1, 3   D. 4, 3, 2, 1

Questions 3-5.

DIRECTIONS: The sentences listed below are part of a meaningful paragraph but they are not given in their proper order. You are to decide what would be the *best order* in which to put the sentences so as to form a well-organized paragraph. Each sentence has a place in the paragraph; there are no extra sentences. You are then to answer questions 3 to 5 inclusive on the basis of your rearrangements of these scrambled sentences into a properly organized paragraph.

In 1887 some insurance companies organized an Inspection Department to advise their clients on all phases of fire prevention and protection. Probably this has been due to the smaller annual fire losses in Great Britain than in the United States. It tests various fire prevention devices and appliances and determines manufacturing hazards and their safeguards. Fire research began earlier in the United States and is more advanced than in Great Britain. Later they established a laboratory specializing in electrical, mechanical, hydraulic, and chemical fields.

3. When the five sentences are arranged in proper order, the paragraph starts with the sentence which begins

    A. "In 1887..."   B. "Probably this ..."   C. "It tests ..."
    D. "Fire research ..."   E. "Later they ..."

3.____

4. In the last sentence listed above, "they" refers to

    A. insurance companies
    B. the United States and Great Britain
    C. the Inspection Department
    D. clients
    E. technicians

4.____

5. When the above paragraph is properly arranged, it ends with the words

    A. "... and protection."   B. "... the United States."
    C. "... their safeguards."   D. "... in Great Britain."
    E. "... chemical fields."

5.____

_____

KEY (CORRECT ANSWERS)

    1. C
    2. C
    3. D
    4. A
    5. C

_____

TEST 2

DIRECTIONS: In each of the questions numbered 1 through 5, several sentences are given. For each question, choose as your answer the group of numbers that represents the *most logical* order of these sentences if they were arranged in paragraph form. *PRINT THE LETTER OF THE CORRECT ANSWER IN THE SPACE AT THE RIGHT.*

1. 1. It is established when one shows that the landlord has prevented the tenant's enjoyment of his interest in the property leased.
    2. Constructive eviction is the result of a breach of the covenant of quiet enjoyment implied in all leases.
    3. In some parts of the United States, it is not complete until the tenant vacates within a reasonable time.
    4. Generally, the acts must be of such serious and permanent character as to deny the tenant the enjoyment of his possessing rights.
    5. In this event, upon abandonment of the premises, the tenant's liability for that ceases.
    The CORRECT answer is:

    A. 2, 1, 4, 3, 5   B. 5, 2, 3, 1, 4   C. 4, 3, 1, 2, 5
    D. 1, 3, 5, 4, 2

1.____

2. 1. The powerlessness before private and public authorities that is the typical experience of the slum tenant is reminiscent of the situation of blue-collar workers all through the nineteenth century.
    2. Similarly, in recent years, this chapter of history has been reopened by anti-poverty groups which have attempted to organize slum tenants to enable them to bargain collectively with their landlords about the conditions of their tenancies.
    3. It is familiar history that many of the workers remedied their condition by joining together and presenting their demands collectively.
    4. Like the workers, tenants are forced by the conditions of modern life into substantial dependence on these who possess great political arid economic power.
    5. What's more, the very fact of dependence coupled with an absence of education and self-confidence makes them hesitant and unable to stand up for what they need from those in power.
    The CORRECT answer is:

    A. 5, 4, 1, 2, 3   B. 2, 3, 1, 5, 4   C. 3, 1, 5, 4, 2
    D. 1, 4, 5, 3, 2

2.____

3. 1. A railroad, for example, when not acting as a common carrier may contract away responsibility for its own negligence.
    2. As to a landlord, however, no decision has been found relating to the legal effect of a clause shifting the statutory duty of repair to the tenant.
    3. The courts have not passed on the validity of clauses relieving the landlord of this duty and liability.
    4. They have, however, upheld the validity of exculpatory clauses in other types of contracts.
    5. Housing regulations impose a duty upon the landlord to maintain leased premises in safe condition.

3.____

6. As another example, a bailee may limit his liability except for gross negligence, willful acts, or fraud.

The CORRECT answer is:

A. 2, 1, 6, 4, 3, 5   B. 1, 3, 4, 5, 6, 2   C. 3, 5, 1, 4, 2, 6
D. 5, 3, 4, 1, 6, 2

4.   1. Since there are only samples in the building, retail or consumer sales are generally   4.____
eschewed by mart occupants, and in some instances, rigid controls are maintained to limit entrance to the mart only to those persons engaged in retailing.
   2. Since World War I, in many larger cities, there has developed a new type of property, called the mart building.
   3. It can, therefore, be used by wholesalers and jobbers for the display of sample merchandise.
   4. This type of building is most frequently a multi-storied, finished interior property which is a cross between a retail arcade and a loft building.
   5. This limitation enables the mart occupants to ship the orders from another location after the retailer or dealer makes his selection from the samples.

The CORRECT answer is:

A. 2, 4, 3, 1, 5   B. 4, 3, 5, 1, 2   C. 1, 3, 2, 4, 5
D. 1, 4, 2, 3, 5

5.   1. In general, staff-line friction reduces the distinctive contribution of staff personnel.   5.____
   2. The conflicts, however, introduce an uncontrolled element into the managerial system.
   3. On the other hand, the natural resistance of the line to staff innovations probably usefully restrains over-eager efforts to apply untested procedures on a large scale.
   4. Under such conditions, it is difficult to know when valuable ideas are being sacrificed.
   5. The relatively weak position of staff, requiring accommodation to the line, tends to restrict their ability to engage in free, experimental innovation.

The CORRECT answer is:

A. 4, 2, 3, 1, 3   B. 1, 5, 3, 2, 4   C. 5, 3, 1, 2, 4
D. 2, 1, 4, 5, 3

———

KEY (CORRECT ANSWERS)

1. A
2. D
3. D
4. A
5. B

———

TEST 3

DIRECTIONS: Questions 1 through 4 consist of six sentences which can be arranged in a logical sequence. For each question, select the choice which places the numbered sentences in the *most logical* sequence. *PRINT THE LETTER OF THE CORRECT ANSWER IN THE SPACE AT THE RIGHT.*

1.   1.   The burden of proof as to each issue is determined before trial and remains upon the same party throughout the trial.   1.____
      2.   The jury is at liberty to believe one witness' testimony as against a number of contradictory witnesses.
      3.   In a civil case, the party bearing the burden of proof is required to prove his contention by a fair preponderance of the evidence.
      4.   However, it must be noted that a fair preponderance of evidence does not necessarily mean a greater number of witnesses.
      5.   The burden of proof is the burden which rests upon one of the parties to an action to persuade the trier of the facts, generally the jury, that a proposition he asserts is true.
      6.   If the evidence is equally balanced, or if it leaves the jury in such doubt as to be unable to decide the controversy either way, judgment must be given against the party upon whom the burden of proof rests.
      The CORRECT answer is:

      A.   3, 2, 5, 4, 1, 6   B.   1, 2, 6, 5, 3, 4   C.   3, 4, 5, 1, 2, 6
      D.   5, 1, 3, 6, 4, 2

2.   1.   If a parent is without assets and is unemployed, he cannot be convicted of the crime of non-support of a child.   2.____
      2.   The term "sufficient ability" has been held to mean sufficient financial ability.
      3.   It does not matter if his unemployment is by choice or unavoidable circumstances.
      4.   If he fails to take any steps at all, he may be liable to prosecution for endangering the welfare of a child.
      5.   Under the penal law, a parent is responsible for the support of his minor child only if the parent is "of sufficient ability."
      6.   An indigent parent may meet his obligation by borrowing money or by seeking aid under the provisions of the Social Welfare Law.
      The CORRECT answer is:

      A.   6, 1, 5, 3, 2, 4   B.   1, 3, 5, 2, 4, 6   C.   5, 2, 1, 3, 6, 4
      D.   1, 6, 4, 5, 2, 3

3.

1. Consider, for example, the case of a rabble rouser who urges a group of twenty people to go out and break the windows of a nearby factory.
2. Therefore, the law fills the indicated gap with the crime of inciting to riot.
3. A person is considered guilty of inciting to riot when he urges ten or more persons to engage in tumultuous and violent conduct of a kind likely to create public alarm.
4. However, if he has not obtained the cooperation of at least four people, he cannot be charged with unlawful assembly.
5. The charge of inciting to riot was added to the law to cover types of conduct which cannot be classified as either the crime of "riot" or the crime of "unlawful assembly."
6. If he acquires the acquiescence of at least four of them, he is guilty of unlawful assembly even if the project does not materialize.

The CORRECT answer is:

A. 3, 5, 1, 6, 4, 2   B. 5, 1, 4, 6, 2, 3   C. 3, 4, 1, 5, 2, 6
D. 5, 1, 4, 6, 3, 2

3._____

4.

1. If, however, the rebuttal evidence presents an issue of credibility, it is for the jury to determine whether the presumption has, in fact, been destroyed.
2. Once sufficient evidence to the contrary is introduced, the presumption disappears from the trial.
3. The effect of a presumption is to place the burden upon the adversary to come forward with evidence to rebut the presumption.
4. When a presumption is overcome and ceases to exist in the case, the fact or facts which gave rise to the presumption still remain.
5. Whether a presumption has been overcome is ordinarily a question for the court.
6. Such information may furnish a basis for a logical inference.

The CORRECT answer is:

A. 4, 6, 2, 5, 1, 3   B. 3, 2, 5, 1, 4, 6   C. 5, 3, 6, 4, 2, 1
D. 5, 4, 1, 2, 6, 3

4._____

KEY (CORRECT ANSWERS)

1. D
2. C
3. A
4. B

PREPARING WRITTEN MATERIAL

EXAMINATION SECTION
TEST 1

DIRECTIONS : Each of the sentences in the tests that follow may be classified under one of the following four categories:

    A. *Incorrect* because of faulty grammar or sentence structure
    B. *Incorrect* because of faulty punctuation
    C. *Incorrect* because of faulty capitalization
    D. *Correct*

Examine each sentence carefully to determine under which of the above four options it is best classified. Then, in the space on the right, print the capital letter preceding the option which is the *BEST* of the four suggested above.

(Each incorrect sentence contains but one type of error. Consider a sentence to be correct if it contains none of the types of errors mentioned, even though there may be other correct ways of expressing the same thought.)

1. This fact, together with those brought out at the previous meeting, prove that the schedule is satisfactory to the employees.   1.____

2. Like many employees in scientific fields, the work of bookkeepers and accountants requires accuracy and neatness.   2.____

3. "What can I do for you," the secretary asked as she motioned to the visitor to take a seat.   3.____

4. Our representative, Mr. Charles will call on you next week to determine whether or not your claim has merit.   4.____

5. We expect you to return in the spring; please do not disappoint us.   5.____

6. Any supervisor, who disregards the just complaints of his subordinates, is remiss in the performance of his duty.   6.____

7. Because she took less than an hour for lunch is no reason for permitting her to leave before five o'clock.   7.____

8. "Miss Smith," said the supervisor, "Please arrange a meeting of the staff for two o'clock on Monday."   8.____

9. A private company's vacation and sick leave allowance usually differs considerably from a public agency.   9.____

10. Therefore, in order to increase the efficiency of operations in the department, a report on the recommended changes in procedures was presented to the departmental committee in charge of the program.   10.____

11. We told him to assign the work to whoever was available.   11.____

12. Since John was the most efficient of any other employee in the bureau, he received the highest service rating.   12.____

13. Only those members of the national organization who resided in the middle West   13.____
attended the conference in Chicago.

14. The question of whether the office manager has as yet attained, or indeed can ever hope   14.____
to secure professional status is one which has been discussed for years.

15. No one knew who to blame for the error which, we later discovered, resulted in a consid-   15.____
erable loss of time.

————

KEY (CORRECT ANSWERS)

1.	A		6.	B
2.	A		7.	A
3.	B		8.	C
4.	B		9.	A
5.	D		10.	D

11.	D
12.	A
13.	C
14.	B
15.	A

————

TEST 2

DIRECTIONS : Each of the sentences in the tests that follow may be classified under one of the following four categories:

        A. *Incorrect* because of faulty grammar or sentence structure
        B. *Incorrect* because of faulty punctuation
        C. *Incorrect* because of faulty capitalization
        D. *Correct*

1. The National alliance of Businessmen is trying to persuade private businesses to hire youth in the summertime.   1.____

2. The supervisor who is on vacation, is in charge of processing vouchers.   2.____

3. The activity of the committee at its conferences is always stimulating.   3.____

4. After checking the addresses again, the letters went to the mailroom.   4.____

5. The director, as well as the employees, are interested in sharing the dividends.   5.____

———

KEY (CORRECT ANSWERS)

1. C
2. B
3. D
4. A
5. A

TEST 3

DIRECTIONS: In each of the following groups of sentences, one of the four sentences is faulty in grammar, punctuation, or capitalization. Select the incorrect sentence in each case.

1. A. Sailing down the bay was a thrilling experience for me.   1.____
    B. He was not consulted about your joining the club.
    C. This story is different than the one I told you yesterday.
    D. There is no doubt about his being the best player.

2. A. He maintains there is but one road to world peace.   2.____
    B. It is common knowledge that a child sees much he is not supposed to see.
    C. Much of the bitterness might have been avoided if arbitration had been resorted to earlier in the meeting.
    D. The man decided it would be advisable to marry a girl somewhat younger than him.

3. A. In this book, the incident I liked least is where the hero tries to put out the forest fire.   3.____
    B. Learning a foreign language will undoubtedly give a person a better understanding of his mother tongue.
    C. His actions made us wonder what he planned to do next.
    D. Because of the war, we were unable to travel during the summer vacation.

4. A. The class had no sooner become interested in the lesson than the dismissal bell rang.   4.____
    B. There is little agreement about the kind of world to be planned at the peace conference.
    C. "Today," said the teacher, "we shall read 'The Wind in the Willows.' I am sure you'll like it.
    D. The terms of the legal settlement of the family quarrel handicapped both sides for many years.

5. A. I was so suprised that I was not able to say a word.   5.____
    B. She is taller than any other member of the class.
    C. It would be much more preferable if you were never seen in his company.
    D. We had no choice but to excuse her for being late.

————

KEY (CORRECT ANSWERS)

1. C
2. D
3. A
4. C
5. C

———

TEST 4

DIRECTIONS: In each of the following groups of sentences, one of the four sentences is faulty in grammar, punctuation, or capitalization. Select the incorrect sentence in each case.

1. A. Please send me these data at the earliest opportunity.   1.____
    B. The loss of their material proved to be a severe handicap.
    C. My principal objection to this plan is that it is impracticable.
    D. The doll had laid in the rain for an hour and was ruined.

2. A. The garden scissors, left out all night in the rain, were in a badly rusted condition.   2.____
    B. The girls felt bad about the misunderstanding which had arisen.
    C. Sitting near the campfire, the old man told John and I about many exciting adventures he had had.
    D. Neither of us is in a position to undertake a task of that magnitude.

3. A. The general concluded that one of the three roads would lead to the besieged city.   3.____
    B. The children didn't, as a rule, do hardly anything beyond what they were told to do.
    C. The reason the girl gave for her negligence was that she had acted on the spur of the moment.
    D. The daffodils and tulips look beautiful in that blue vase.

4. A. If I was ten years older, I should be interested in this work.   4.____
    B. Give the prize to whoever has drawn the best picture.
    C. When you have finished reading the book, take it back to the library.
    D. My drawing is as good as or better than yours.

5. A. He asked me whether the substance was animal or vegetable.   5.____
    B. An apple which is unripe should not be eaten by a child.
    C. That was an insult to me who am your friend.
    D. Some spy must of reported the matter to the enemy.

6. A. Limited time makes quoting the entire message impossible.   6.____
    B. Who did she say was going?
    C. The girls in your class have dressed more dolls this year than we.
    D. There was such a large amount of books on the floor that I couldn't find a place for my rocking chair.

7. A. What with his sleeplessness and his ill health, he was unable to assume any responsibility for the success of the meeting.   7.____
    B. If I had been born in February, I should be celebrating my birthday soon.
    C. In order to prevent breakage, she placed a sheet of paper between each of the plates when she packed them.
    D. After the spring shower, the violets smelled very sweet.

8. A. He had laid the book down very reluctantly before the end of the lesson.   8.____
    B. The dog, I am sorry to say, had lain on the bed all night.
    C. The cloth was first lain on a flat surface; then it was pressed with a hot iron.
    D. While we were in Florida, we lay in the sun until we were noticeably tanned.

9.   A.   If John was in New York during the recent holiday season, I have no doubt he spent   9.____
            most of his time with his parents.
      B.   How could he enjoy the television program; the dog was barking and the baby
            was crying.
      C.   When the problem was explained to the class, he must have been asleep.
      D.   She wished that her new dress were finished so that she could go to the party.

10.   A.   The engine not only furnishes power but light and heat as well.   10.____
      B.   You're aware that we've forgotten whose guilt was established, aren't you?
      C.   Everybody knows that the woman made many sacrifices for her children.
      D.   A man with his dog and gun is a familiar sight in this neighborhood.

KEY (CORRECT ANSWERS)

1.	D		6.	D
2.	C		7.	B
3.	B		8.	C
4.	A		9.	B
5.	D		10.	A

TEST 5

DIRECTIONS: Each of Questions 1 to 15 consists of a sentence which may be classified appropriately under one of the following four categories:
A. *Incorrect* because of faulty grammar
B. *Incorrect* because of faulty punctuation
C. *Incorrect* because of faulty spelling
D. *Correct*

Examine each sentence carefully. Then, print, in the space on the right, the letter preceding the category which is the best of the four suggested above.

(Note: Each incorrect sentence contains only one type of error. Consider a sentence correct if it contains no errors, although there may be other correct ways of writing the sentence.)

1. Of the two employees, the one in our office is the most efficient.   1._____

2. No one can apply or even understand, the new rules and regulations.   2._____

3. A large amount of supplies were stored in the empty office.   3._____

4. If an employee is occassionally asked to work overtime, he should do so willingly.   4._____

5. It is true that the new procedures are difficult to use but, we are certain that you will learn them quickly.   5._____

6. The office manager said that he did not know who would be given a large allotment under the new plan.   6._____

7. It was at the supervisor's request that the clerk agreed to postpone his vacation.   7._____

8. We do not believe that it is necessary for both he and the clerk to attend the conference.   8._____

9. All employees, who display perseverance, will be given adequate recognition.   9._____

10. He regrets that some of us employees are dissatisfied with our new assignments.   10._____

11. "Do you think that the raise was merited," asked the supervisor?   11._____

12. The new manual of procedure is a valuable supplament to our rules and regulations.   12._____

13. The typist admitted that she had attempted to pursuade the other employees to assist her in her work.   13._____

14. The supervisor asked that all amendments to the regulations be handled by you and I.   14._____

15. The custodian seen the boy who broke the window.   15._____

KEY (CORRECT ANSWERS)

1.	A		6.	D
2.	B		7.	D
3.	A		8.	A
4.	C		9.	B
5.	B		10.	D

11.	B
12.	C
13.	C
14.	A
15.	A

———

Made in United States
North Haven, CT
18 May 2022

19299805R00117